# TALES OF THE GREEN LANTERN CORPS

## selected by GEOFF JOHNS



Cover art by Jim Lee & Scott Williams
Publication design by Joseph DiStefano

GREEN LANTERN: IN BRIGHTEST DAY
Published by DC Comics. 

DC Comics, 1700 Broadway, New York, NY 10019.
A Warner Bros. Entertainment Company. Printed in Canada. First Printing.
ISBN: 978-1-4012-1986-4

# INTRODUCTION

Under the editorial guidance of Julius Schwartz, John Broome and Gil Kane reinvented the concept of Green Lantern at the dawn of DC's Silver Age. They introduced test pilot Hal Jordan and the intergalactic police force known as the Green Lantern Corps.

I wasn't around when Hal Jordan first appeared. In fact, I didn't discover Green Lantern until nearly three decades after his first appearance. But those issues of Green Lantern by John Broome and Gil Kane were among the first I read. My brother and I discovered them in my grandmother's attic twenty-six years after they were published. From there, we found comic books at the drugstore and we were surprised to find out that the daredevil, take-no-prisoners Hal Jordan was no longer the Green Lantern of Earth. A proactive bad-ass named John Stewart was. That's the beauty of a universe full of ring-slinging cops. There's lots of them.

I was introduced to Kilowog, the Green Lantern Corps' drill sergeant; Guy Gardner, another Earthman, obsessed with being chosen second to Jordan; the Guardians of the Universe, the immortals who established and oversaw the Corps and dozens of other alien officers and their enemies...including a character I've gravitated towards in my own work on Green Lantern, the renegade Sinestro.

In 2003, I had the opportunity to rebuild Green Lantern. Hal Jordan had been literally dead and buried, but under the editorial guidance of Paul Levitz, Dan DiDio and my personal Guardian of the Universe, Peter Tomasi, I was able to resurrect him in GREEN LANTERN: REBIRTH alongside the genius who redefined the visuals of the Lanterns, Ethan Van Sciver. I've been fortunate enough to continue writing GREEN LANTERN, working with some brilliant collaborators: Dave Gibbons, Carlos Pacheco and the king of willpower himself, Ivan Reis.

I have to give a special shout-out to Dave, but I'll be doing that later in this collection.

I was asked if I'd be interested in creating a collection of what I consider the most important and most influential tales of Hal Jordan and the Green Lantern Corps, i.e., the "greatest Green Lantern stories ever told" from my point of view. Some of these changed Green Lantern mythology forever, and some of them are simply favorites. A lot of them f eature the origins or beginnings of characters and concepts within the work I'm currently doing. Many have elements that will play into my upcoming storyline, GREEN LANTERN: THE BLACKEST NIGHT.

The adventures within the following pages were crafted by an extremely talented group of writers and artists. Some, like Broome and Kane and Alan Moore and Dave Gibbons, are well known for their contributions. Others, like Todd Klein and Joey Cavalieri and Kevin O'Neill, added far more to the mythos than most might realize.

– Geoff Johns

# THE DAY 100,000 PEOPLE VANISHED

**Writer:** JOHN BROOME **Penciller:** GIL KANE **Inker:** JOE GIELLA

Originally presented in GREEN LANTERN No. 7, July - August 1961

There is always a beginning. And for me, the introduction of Sinestro, the renegade Green Lantern, in GREEN LANTERN #7 by John Broome and Gil Kane marked the beginning of the complexities that would be revealed and built upon within what, to me, is the greatest mythology in modern day comic books. The idea of a "cop gone bad" on an intergalactic level opened up more doors for where Hal Jordan would eventually go than I think anyone ever realized. And the introduction of a being who represented everything Hal Jordan wasn't, and everything he struggled not to be, laid the groundwork for one of the most compelling and frightening villains within the DC Universe.

And did you know when Sinestro first appeared as the renegade Green Lantern, he didn't wield a yellow ring? Weird, huh?

– Geoff Johns

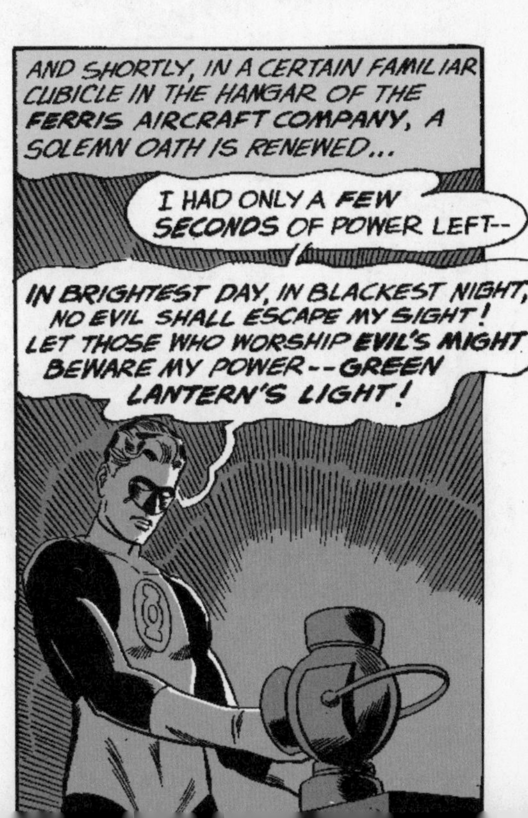

GREEN LANTERN
THE INCREDIBLE OCCURRENCE IN VALDALE, AN ORDINARILY BUSY COMMUNITY ON THE WEST COAST, LED GREEN LANTERN, STALWART CHAMPION OF JUSTICE, ON A LONG, LONG TRAIL THAT FINALLY BROUGHT HIM FACE TO FACE WITH A FANTASTIC FOE -- THE AMAZING SINESTRO, A RENEGADE "GREEN LANTERN" WHO HAD JOINED FORCES WITH THE EVIL WEAPONERS OF QWARD!
IT'S UNCANNY! EVERY SINGLE PERSON IN THIS CITY SEEMS TO HAVE VANISHED OFF THE FACE OF THE EARTH!
The DAY 100,000 PEOPLE VANISHED!
GREEN LANTERN-- YOU'RE NEXT!

T PRECISELY FOURTEEN MINUTES AFTER NINE ON A BRIGHT MORNING IN THE THRIVING COMMUNITY F VALDALE ON THE WEST COAST, THE RESIDENTS BUSTLE ABOUT THEIR USUAL ACTIVITIES...
FILL 'ER UP, JOE!
GET A MOVE ON, WILLYA?
LOVELY DAY, ISN'T IT, MRS. WILSON?
HONK!

UDDENLY, THERE IS AN ODD SHIMMERING N THE AIR, LIKE A RAIN OF LIGHT...

AND THE NEXT INSTANT A NOISE LIKE A THUNDERCLAP...
CRACK!

AND AT EXACTLY NINE FIFTEEN, ONE MINUTE LATER, THE CITY OF VALDALE, 100,000 STRONG...
...HAS BECOME A GHOST TOWN WITH NOT A SINGLE LIVING HUMAN BEING LEFT IN IT!
2.

WHAT IS THE MEANING OF THIS EXTRA-ORDINARY EVENT WHICH HORRIFIES THE ENTIRE NATION WHEN IT BECOMES KNOWN? IT IS A MYSTERY WHICH BAFFLES GREEN LANTERN-- ALIAS HAL JORDAN, ACE TEST PILOT--AS MUCH AS ANYONE...

GREEN LANTERN-- DID YOU FIND OUT WHAT HAPPENED AT VALDALE?

I EXAMINED THE WHOLE TOWN WITH MY POWER RING, PIEFACE--THER NOT A SINGLE CLUE! THE PEOPLE ARE GONE AS IF THEY VANISHED INTO THIN AIR!
JUMPING FISHHOOKS!

WHILE ON THE WAY BACK FROM VALDALE, I WAS THINKING-- THE INCREDIBLE DISAPPEARANCE TOOK PLACE AT A LITTLE AFTER NINE O'CLOCK...
THAT'S RIGH GL! BUT WHAT--?

PIEFACE, IT JUST HAPPENS THAT I WAS SUPPOSED TO BE IN VALDALE AT THAT HOUR--TO TAKE PART IN A CEREMONY OPENING UP A NEW BOYS SETTLEMENT HOUSE THERE! I COULDN'T MAKE IT BECAUSE I HAD TO FINISH A CASE I WAS WORK-ING ON...

GREAT AURORA! THEN YOU WOULD HAVE VANISHED TOO--IF YOU HAD KEPT THE APPOINT-MENT!
EXACTLY! AND I CAN'T HELP WON-DERING-- EH?

BEFORE THE EMERALD GLADIATOR CAN CONTINUE, AN ODD FEELING PASSES OVER HIM...
THAT'S STRANGE FOR AN INSTANT MY MIND WENT BLANK AND I COULDN'T REMEM-BER WHAT I WAS SAYING! BUT I'M OKAY NOW!

T THAT "BLANK" MOMENT, UNKNOWN TO GREEN LANTERN,

EANWHILE, ON THE FAR-FLUNG WORLD OF
A, IN THE CENTRAL GALAXY OF THE
NIVERSE, WHERE A GROUP KNOWN SIMPLY
S THE GUARDIANS SITS IN COUNCIL...

HE ENERGY-DUPLICATE OF THE POWER
BATTERY POSSESSOR IN SECTOR 2814
IS ON THE WAY HERE!

AS A BURST OF LIGHT FLARED BEFORE THE IMPRESSIVE ASSEMBLAGE...
THE--THE GUARDIANS OF THE UNIVERSE!
YES! YOUR ENERGY-TWIN REMEMBERS WHAT YOUR CONSCIOUS MIND BACK ON EARTH IS STILL UNAWARE OF, GREEN LANTERN--THAT WE ARE THE CREATORS OF POWER BATTERIES SUCH AS YOURS...

.AND THAT ONCE BEFORE WE SUMMONED YOU TO US IN A GREAT EMERGENCY! BUT NE HAVE NOT BROUGHT YOU HERE THIS TIME TO TALK ABOUT OURSELVES--BUT RATHER OF A SITUATION THAT THREATENS YOU!
THREATENS-- ME?

WE GUARDIANS DO NOT BESTOW POWER BATTERIES WITHOUT CAREFUL TESTS! BUT THERE ARE MANY POSSESSORS AND MANY WORLDS IN THE COSMOS UNDER OUR CARE! AND IN OUR SELECTIONS WE DID MAKE ONE MISTAKE! IT HAPPENED...

"...ON A WORLD CALLED KORUGAR IN SECTOR 1417 WHERE WE CHOSE A BEING NAMED SINESTRO..."
"...TO BE THE POSSESSOR OF A POWER BATTERY!"
4

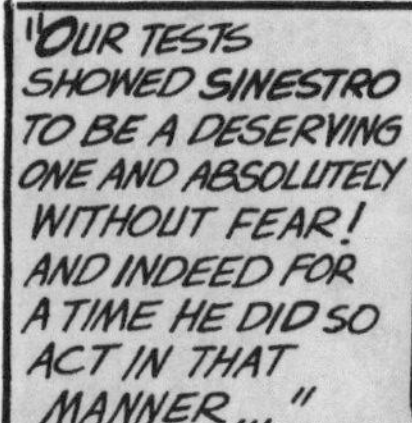
"OUR TESTS SHOWED SINESTRO TO BE A DESERVING ONE AND ABSOLUTELY WITHOUT FEAR! AND INDEED FOR A TIME HE DID SO ACT IN THAT MANNER..."

SINESTRO IS KEEPING DOWN EVIL ON HIS PLANET!

"BUT IN DUE COURSE, AFTER ONE OF OUR PERIODIC CHECKS, A SUBTLE CHANGE CAME OVER THE KORUGARN GREEN LANTERN WHICH WE WERE THEN UNAWARE OF..."
CHARGING MY RING AT THE BATTERY GIVES ME POWER FOR 37 DIORS*--UNLIMITED POWER! THERE IS NOTHING I CAN'T DO WITH IT!
*Editor's Note: THE EQUIVALENT OF 24 EARTH-HOURS!

"A FEELING OF DISSATISFACTION FILLED SINESTRO AS HE STARED ABOUT HIM..."
WHY SHOULD I REMAIN IN THIS SECRET CHAMBER--HIDDEN HERE FROM MY WORLD? I HAVE A BETTER IDEA--AND A SENSATIONAL WAY TO EMPLOY MY RING!

"USING HIS POWER BEAM, SINESTRO CREATED A SUMPTUOUS HEADQUARTERS FOR HIMSELF, OUTSHINING EVERYTHING ELSE ON HIS PLANET..."
THERE! NOW I HAVE SUITABLE HEADQUARTERS--THE MOST MARVELOUS BUILDING ON KORUGAR!

"FROM THEN ON, THIS GREEN LANTERN DISPENSED JUSTICE FROM HIS NEW HEADQUARTERS! BUT IN A STRANGE WAY..."
EVIL RAIDERS THREATENING YOUR SETTLEMENT--ROBBING YOU?
HOW I AM BORED WITH THESE DIORDAN-LONG COMPLAINTS AND PLEAS FOR MY ASSISTANCE!
WE HAVE TO WAIT TO SEE SINESTRO SOMETIMES FOR DIORDANS*!
AND THEN HE TAKES ONLY THOSE CASES THAT INTEREST HIM--HELPS ONLY A FEW OF US AND IGNORES THE REST!
*Editor's Note: DIORDAN: 37 DIORS, OR ONE DAY!

LTHOUGH SINESTRO DID NOT REALIZE IT, HE WAS ALREADY INFECTED WITH THE VIRUS OF POWER--TO WHICH, BY A PSYCHOLOGICAL QUIRK IN HIS BRAIN, HE DID NOT HAVE ENOUGH RESISTANCE! AND FROM THEN IT WAS JUST A SHORT STEP TO HIS NEXT ACT...
"ONE OF THE SUPPLICANTS WHOM HE HAD REFUSED TO HELP RE-MONSTRATED WITH HIM, CHARGED HIM WITH LACK OF GOOD WILL..."
YOU ARE NO CHAMPION OF JUSTICE! WE HEARD GREEN LANTERN WOULD CRUSH EVIL WHEN IT THREATENED US! BUT INSTEAD YOU HAVE BECOME POWER-MAD!
YOU DARE--!?
"WITH ONE BURST OF HIS RING, THE KORUGARN GREEN LANTERN STRUCK THE SPEAKER UNCONSCIOUS...
FOR SHAME! KI-MON WAS UNARMED--HELPLESS!
SILENCE! OR ALL OF YOU WILL GET THE SAME TREATMENT! I AM GREEN LANTERN--NO ONE CAN TELL ME WHAT TO DO!
"PRIDE AND A LOVE OF POWER WERE SINESTRO'S UNDOING! SOON IN THE GOV-ERNING BODY OF HIS WORLD..."
SINCE I HAVE DECIDED TO GOVERN KORUGAR MYSELF, I HEREBY DISSOLVE THE HIGH COUNCIL!
HE IS MAKING HIMSELF DICTATOR!
"A PALL FELL OVER KORUGAR! NONE KNEW WHEN HE MIGHT INCUR THE NEW MASTER'S DISPLEASURE..."
THREE WHO SPOKE AGAINST GREEN LANTERN THE OTHER DIORDAN HAVE DISAPPEARED!
HE HAS BECOME A LAW UNTO HIMSELF! WE ARE ENSLAVED!
"BUT FORTUNATELY AT THIS TIME WE GUARDIANS MADE ONE OF OUR PERIODIC SECRET CHECKS..."
SINESTRO HAS MIS-USED THE POWER WE BESTOWED ON HIM!
HE BELIEVED THAT NONE STOOD ABOVE HIM! HE WILL NOW LEARN THAT HE WAS MISTAKEN!
6

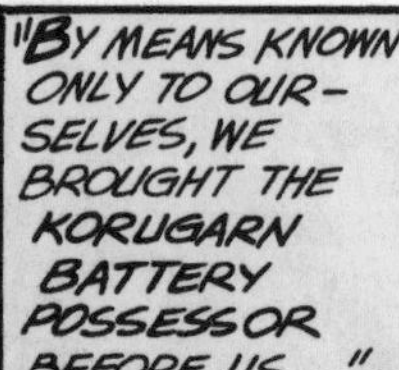
"BY MEANS KNOWN ONLY TO OUR-SELVES, WE BROUGHT THE KORUGARN BATTERY POSSESSOR BEFORE US..."

SINESTRO, YOU HAVE ABUSED YOUR SACRED TRUST! INSTEAD OF DISPENSING JUSTICE ON YOUR WORLD--YOU HAVE DIS-PENSED EVIL! UNDER THE CIRCUMSTANCES THERE IS ONLY ONE COURSE OPEN TO US!

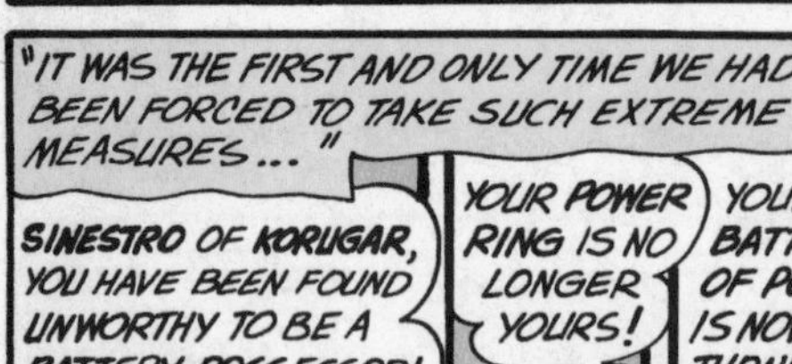
"IT WAS THE FIRST AND ONLY TIME WE HAD BEEN FORCED TO TAKE SUCH EXTREME MEASURES..."

SINESTRO OF KORUGAR, YOU HAVE BEEN FOUND UNWORTHY TO BE A BATTERY POSSESSOR! YOU ARE HEREBY STRIPPED OF ALL INSIGNIA AND HONORS--!

YOUR POWER RING IS NO LONGER YOURS!

YOUR BATTERY OF POWER IS NOW RE-TURNING TO US!

EVIL YOU ARE--TO EVIL YOU WILL GO! WE ARE BANISHING YOU TO THE ANTIMATTER UNIVERSE OF QWARD--WHERE ALL IS EVIL AND WHERE YOUR EVIL WILL FIND ONLY OTHER EVIL TO CLASH WITH!

"WE THOUGHT THAT BY SENDING SINESTRO OUT OF OUR UNIVERSE ALTOGETHER WE HAD ENDED HIS MENACE TO US..."
BUT ONCE AGAIN WE WERE WRONG AS FAR AS SINESTRO WAS CONCERNED! WHICH LEADS US TO WHY WE BROUGHT YOU HERE TODAY!

THOUGH WE HAVE NO POWER IN THE ANTI-MATTER UNIVERSE OF QWARD, WE CAN PEER INTO IT! NOW WE WILL SHOW YOU CERTAIN SCENES WHICH OUR DEVICES HAVE RE-CORDED--SCENES OF INTEREST TO YOU!

"SINESTRO WITH HIS FIERY ENERGY LOST NO TIME IN CONTACTING THE RULERS OF HIS NEW UNIVERSE--THE EVIL WEAPONERS OF QWARD..."
I AM DETERMINED TO BECOME MASTER OF THIS WORLD JUST AS I WAS MASTER OF KORUGAR! THE GUARDIANS WILL NEVER SHAKE MY WILL! I SHALL DEFEAT THEM YET! AND THERE IS ONE WAY TO BEGIN MY STRUGGLE--

"THE QWARDIANS WERE AWED BY SINESTRO! THEY AGREED EAGERLY TO COOPERATE WITH HIM AND GIVE HIM CERTAIN MATERIALS HE ASKED FOR..."

UNDERSTAND, WEAPONERS, THAT GREEN LANTERN CANNOT BE HARMED WHILE HIS POWER RING IS OPERATING! THEREFORE I HAVE CONSTRUCTED THIS MECHANISM--A TRULY EVIL MECHANISM!

Y SUPER-RADAR WE IN QWARD CAN DETECT WHAT IS HAPPENING ON EARTH--EVEN THOUGH WE CANNOT SEE DIRECTLY INTO IT! I HAVE EARNED THAT GREEN LANTERN IS DUE TO APPEAR IN THE CITY OF VALDALE ON EARTH! DURING THAT TIME HIS RING WILL NOT BE OPERATING!

AT THE RIGHT MOMENT I WILL SWITCH ON MY NEW VISO-TELEPORTER--WHICH IS DIRECTED AT VALDALE--AND EVERY VISIBLE HUMAN BEING IN THE CITY--INCLUDING GREEN LANTERN, WILL INSTANTLY BE TRANSPORTED HERE TO QWARD!

MARVELOUS, SINESTRO! WE WILL HAVE GREEN LANTERN IN OUR POWER!

AS THE SCREEN FADES, AND REALIZATION DAWNS ON THE ASTRAL VISITANT...

GREAT STARS! THEN **THAT** EXPLAINS WHAT HAPPENED TO THE PEOPLE OF **VALDALE**! AND I ESCAPED ONLY BY ACCIDENT--BY NOT GOING THERE!

YES! AND NOW THAT WE HAVE TOLD YOU ALL WE KNOW, **GREEN LANTERN** OF EARTH...

...THE REST IS UP TO YOU! YOU MUST DEFEAT YOUR NEW AND VENOMOUS FOE, **SINESTRO**--AND YOU MUST DO IT BY YOURSELF! FOR OUR JURISDICTION DOES NOT EXTEND TO **QWARD** AND WE CANNOT HELP YOU!

I UNDERSTAND! I WILL DO MY BEST!

GOOD! YOU WILL RETURN TO EARTH NOW TO REJOIN YOUR CORPOREAL BODY! BUT THIS TIME, IN RECOGNITION OF YOUR VALOR AND LOYALTY, WE ARE ALLOWING YOU TO RETAIN A COMPLETE MEMORY OF THIS INTERVIEW WITH US!
BACK ON EARTH, ALMOST INSTANTLY, AT THE FERRIS AIRCRAFT COMPANY...
GREEN LANTERN--ARE YOU SURE YOU'RE ALL RIGHT?
YES... YES!
I CAN'T TELL PIEFACE ANYTHING ABOUT THE GUARDIANS! THAT'S ONE SECRET I CAN'T SHARE WITH ANYONE!
THE NEXT MOMENT...
JUMPING FISHHOOKS! HE--HE JUST MUMBLED A FEW WORDS TO ME, AND THEN TOOK OFF--LIKE A STREAK--!

I'VE GOT TO FIND MY WAY INTO QWARD WITHOUT A MOMENT'S DELAY! NOT ONLY MUST SINESTRO BE DEALT WITH--BUT ALSO I'VE GOT TO DISCOVER WHAT HAPPENED TO THE 100,000 INNOCENT PEOPLE OF VALDALE!
9

SHORTLY, AT A CERTAIN HILLSIDE NOT FAR FROM COAST CITY...
Eh? AT THIS SPOT THERE WAS AN INTER-UNIVERSE APERTURE WHICH I USED TO ENTER QWARD-- BUT NOW IT'S BLOCKED--SEALED UP! THAT MUST BE PART OF SINESTRO'S WORK--TO PREVENT A SURPRISE ATTACK ON MY PART!
AS FURTHER SEARCH FAILS TO REVEAL ANY OTHER MEANS OF ACCESS INTO THE ANTI-MATTER UNIVERSE...
THERE'S ONE OTHER WAY TO GET INTO QWARD! IT'S TRICKY-- AND MAYBE DANGEROUS! BUT I'VE GOT TO TRY IT...!

BACK IN COAST CITY, THE VIBRANT CRUSADER UNDERTAKES AN INCREDIBLE MISSION...
THESE PEOPLE WILL ONLY BE AFFECTED TEMPORARILY! BUT MEANWHILE-- I'VE GOT TO USE MY RING TO TURN EVERY LIVING BEING IN THE CITY INVISIBLE--SO THAT THEY WILL BE INVULNERABLE TO SINESTRO'S VISO-TELEPORTER!
WH-WHAT'S HAPPENED TO ME?!

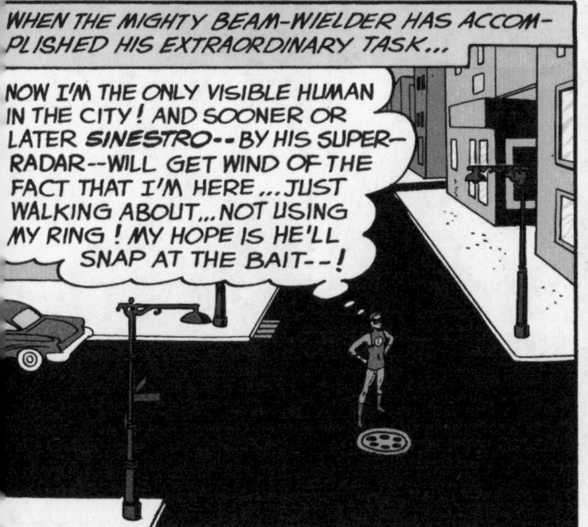
WHEN THE MIGHTY BEAM-WIELDER HAS ACCOMPLISHED HIS EXTRAORDINARY TASK...
NOW I'M THE ONLY VISIBLE HUMAN IN THE CITY! AND SOONER OR LATER SINESTRO--BY HIS SUPER-RADAR--WILL GET WIND OF THE FACT THAT I'M HERE...JUST WALKING ABOUT...NOT USING MY RING! MY HOPE IS HE'LL SNAP AT THE BAIT--!

AFTER WHAT SEEMS AN INTERMINABLE WAIT...
CRRAAACK!
A--AN INCREDIBLE FORCE SEIZING ME! BUT I MUSTN'T RESIST--MUST LET MYSELF GO! IT'S THE ONLY WAY I CAN GET INTO QWARD--!
10

AS THE GREEN-CLAD FIGURE VANISHES, IN THE CITY BEHIND HIM...
IT'S UNCANNY! I--I'M INVISIBLE--AND SO IS EVERYONE ELSE IN TOWN! I'M AFRAID TO DRIVE ANOTHER INCH!

THEN SUDDENLY, SINCE GREEN LANTERN HAD COMMANDED HIS RING TO HAVE ONLY A TEMPORARY EFFECT...
GREAT SCOTT! NOW--NOW WE'RE VISIBLE AGAIN!

AT THIS MOMENT, IN THE ANTI-MATTER UNIVERSE OF QWARD, WHERE EVIL IS THE STANDARD OF BEHAVIOR--JUST AS GOOD IS IN OURS...
SINESTRO HAS KEPT HIS PROMISE! HE HAS DELIVERED GREEN LANTERN TO US!
OPEN FIRE! DESTROY HIM!

AS A BATTERY OF DEADLY RADIATION SPURTS AT THE GREEN CLAD ARRIVAL...
THEY WERE READY FOR ME! I GUESS THEY COUNTED ON MY BEING DAZED WHEN I GOT HERE--UNABLE TO USE MY POWER RING! BUT THEY DON'T REALIZE I FORE-SAW THIS!
ZZZZT!

IN A SPLIT-SECOND, THE GREEN GLADIATOR SETS UP AN IM-PENETRABLE SHIELD BEFORE HIM...
OUR ENERGY BURSTS CAN-NOT REACH HIM! WHAT DO WE DO NOW, SINESTRO?
FEAR NOT! MY EVIL MIND IS EASILY EQUAL TO THIS EMERGENCY--!

HEAR ME, GREEN LANTER UNLESS YOU SURRENDE TO US, YOUR COUNTRY-MEN--THE 100,000 PEOPLE OF VALDALE--WILL BE DESTROYED AT ONCE!

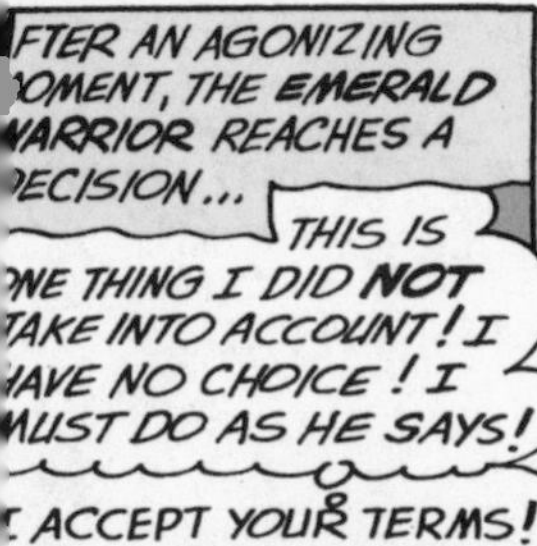
FTER AN AGONIZING
OMENT, THE EMERALD
WARRIOR REACHES A
DECISION...
THIS IS
ONE THING I DID NOT
TAKE INTO ACCOUNT! I
HAVE NO CHOICE! I
MUST DO AS HE SAYS!
I ACCEPT YOUR TERMS!
I WILL PLACE MYSELF
IN YOUR POWER--ON
ONE CONDITION--

--THAT YOU
RELEASE
THE PEOPLE
OF VALDALE,
AND SEND
THEM BACK
WHERE THEY
BELONG--
SAFE AND
SOUND!
AGREED! YOU
HAVE MADE A
GOOD BARGAIN,
GREEN LANTERN--
100,000 FOR
ONE!

AND SOON, BACK IN VALDALE WHICH
WAS A MOMENT BEFORE ONLY A GHOST
CITY...
WH-WHAT
HAPPENED
TO US?
NO ONE KNOWS! BUT THANK
GOODNESS WE ARE BACK
HOME AGAIN AND ALIVE!

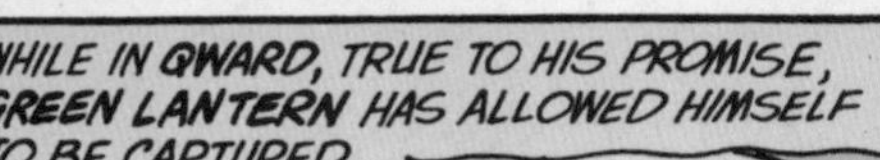
WHILE IN QWARD, TRUE TO HIS PROMISE,
GREEN LANTERN HAS ALLOWED HIMSELF
TO BE CAPTURED...

YOU'VE ENCASED
ME IN A YELLOW
BUBBLE OF PUL-
SATING ENERGY,
SINESTRO! BUT--
IS THIS THE WAY
YOU PROPOSE
TO DESTROY
ME?

PATIENCE, MY
EX-COLLEAGUE--
PATIENCE!

AS A FORMER RING-WIELDER
MYSELF, I KNOW THAT YOUR
GREEN BEAM WILL AUTO-
MATICALLY PROTECT YOU
FROM ALL HARM AS LONG
AS YOU ARE CONSCIOUS!
THEREFORE, MY PLAN IS
SIMPLE! YOU CANNOT
ESCAPE FROM OUR
YELLOW ENERGO-SAC--!*

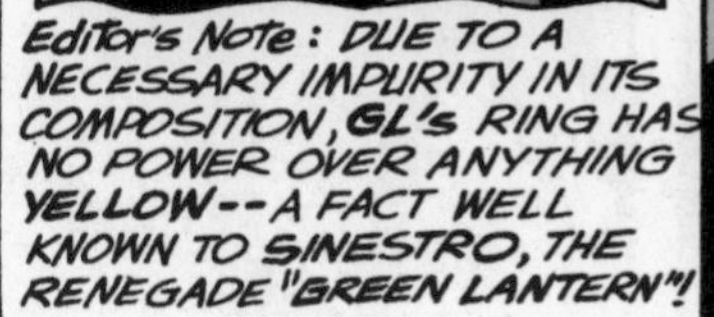
Editor's Note: DUE TO A
NECESSARY IMPURITY IN ITS
COMPOSITION, GL's RING HAS
NO POWER OVER ANYTHING
YELLOW--A FACT WELL
KNOWN TO SINESTRO, THE
RENEGADE "GREEN LANTERN"!

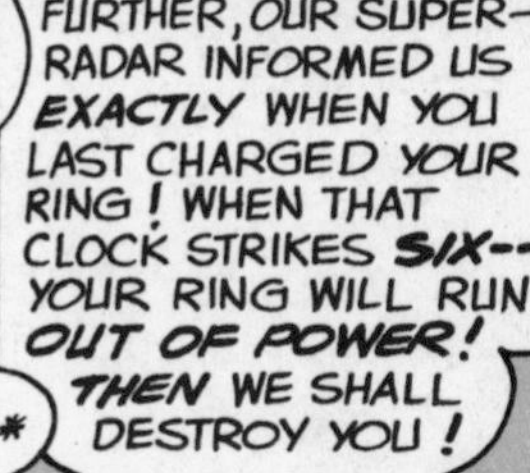
FURTHER, OUR SUPER-
RADAR INFORMED US
EXACTLY WHEN YOU
LAST CHARGED YOUR
RING! WHEN THAT
CLOCK STRIKES SIX--
YOUR RING WILL RUN
OUT OF POWER!
THEN WE SHALL
DESTROY YOU!

12

AS THE MINUTES TICK BY WITH MEASURED AND DREADFUL PACE...
SINESTRO, YOU TRULY ARE A GENIUS OF EVIL! WE HAVE DECIDED TO MAKE YOU OUR CHIEFTAIN!
I ACCEPT! AND AFTER GREEN LANTERN IS FINISHED I SHALL LEAD YOU ON A COUNTERCRUSADE AGAINST MY ETERNAL ENEMIES--THE GUARDIANS!
I MUST ESCAPE FROM HERE AND PREVENT SINESTRO'S ATTACK ON THE GUARDIANS! BUT HOW CAN I? MY RING WON'T PENETRATE THIS YELLOW SURFACE...!

IT SEEMS HOPELESS! AND YET--IN THE TIME I'VE BEEN IN HERE, I'VE NOTICED SOMETHING ABOUT THAT CLOCK! IT WORKS ON THE VIBRATION OF ATOMIC PARTICLES--MY RING HAS BEEN RECEIVING ITS IMPULSES! *Hmm!* I WONDER--!

NOT LONG AFTER, WHEN THE FINAL MOMENT ARRIVES...

THE CLOCK STRIKES SIX!

AND SEE--HIS RING IS RUNNING OUT OF POWER--JUST AS I SAID IT WOULD!

AS THE MASTER OF EVIL UNLIMBERS AN ENERGY-GUN...

NO NEED FOR THE YELLOW BUBBLE, GREEN LANTERN! YOUR HOUR OF DOOM HAS STRUCK--

PERHAPS, SINESTRO...

ZZIT!

...AND PERHAPS NOT!
AHH--!? HIS RING--IT IS STILL WORKING!?

RESSING HIS DVANTAGE, GREEN ANTERN URLS HIM-ELF AT HIS TARTLED FOE...
IMPOSSIBLE--!
NO, SINESTRO! I KNEW I HAD ONLY ONE SLIM CHANCE TO DEFEAT YOUR DIABOLIC SCHEME--BUT IT WAS A CHANCE THAT WORKED!! YOU SEE--
MY RING COULD NOT PIERCE OUR YELLOW BUBBLE, UT I DISCOVERED ONE HING THAT COULD GET UT--THE SUBPARTICLES F CARBON DIOXIDE FROM MY OWN BREATH! AND WHAT I DID WAS O USE MY GREEN BEAM...
"TO PROPEL THE INVISIBLE $CO_2$ PARTICLES OUT OF THE BUBBLE AT THE CLOCK..."
THEY DON'T SUSPECT WHAT I'M UP TO! BUT IF I'M RIGHT, THESE PARTICLES I'M SHOOTING AT THE CLOCK WILL SPEED UP ITS ATOMIC MECHANISM--AND MAKE IT RUN FAST!
AS THE EARTH-CHAMPION PINS HIS ADVERSARY HELPLESSLY TO A WALL...
SO YOU SEE I STILL HAVE PLENTY OF POWER LEFT IN MY RING! ENOUGH TO TAKE CARE OF YOU, SINESTRO, AND YOUR ALLIES--THESE EVIL-SERVING MINIONS OF QWARD! THIS WILL HOLD YOU WHILE I DEAL WITH THEM!
BEFORE THE QWARDIANS CAN RECOVER FROM THEIR SHOCK, A GIGANTIC GREEN WAVE SWEEPS THEM AWAY WITH TITANIC FORCE...
I MUST HURRY! ALTHOUGH I MADE THE CLOCK RUN FAST, I DO NOT HAVE TOO MUCH TIME LEFT OUT OF MY TWENTY-FOUR HOURS OF RING POWER! AND I MUST NOT BE CAUGHT HERE IN THIS ANTIMATTER UNIVERSE WITH AN UNCHARGED RING!
14

AS GREEN LANTERN TURNS ONCE AGAIN TO HIS TRAPPED ARCHFOE...
LAUGHING--!?
HA! HA! OF COURSE! YOU AMUSE ME, GREEN LANTERN, AND I WILL TELL YOU WHY! IF I HAD CAUGHT YOU THE WAY YOU HAVE CAUGHT ME, I WOULD HAVE DESTROYED YOU AT ONCE! BUT YOU--

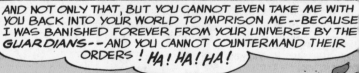

YOUR STUPID CODE PREVENTS YOU FROM KILLING OR HARMING ANYONE IF YOU CAN HELP IT! I KNOW THAT BECAUSE I WORE A UNIFORM LIKE YOURS MYSELF ONCE--BEFORE I LEARNED BETTER! GOOD IS HELPLESS--EVIL ALONE CAN ACT!

AND NOT ONLY THAT, BUT YOU CANNOT EVEN TAKE ME WITH YOU BACK INTO YOUR WORLD TO IMPRISON ME--BECAUSE I WAS BANISHED FOREVER FROM YOUR UNIVERSE BY THE GUARDIANS--AND YOU CANNOT COUNTERMAND THEIR ORDERS! HA! HA! HA!
THAT'S TRUE...

BUT YOU ARE WRONG ABOUT GOOD BEING HELPLESS, SINESTRO! I WILL SHOW YOU HOW WRONG...

ONCE AGAIN THE GREAT GREEN BEAM FLARES OUT WITH INVINCIBLE FORCE, AND INSTANT LATER...
NO FORCE ON QWARD CAN PENETRATE THE RING-MADE BUBBLE I HAVE CAST AROUND YOU, SINESTRO! ANY EVIL YOU CREATE NOW CAN ONLY BE AGAINST YOURSELF! AND WITH THAT PARTING THOUGHT, I BID YOU A FINAL FAREWELL...!

T THE SEALED-UP PERTURE BETWEEN THE TWO NIVERSES SOON AFTER...
I COULDN'T GET THROUGH THIS OPENING FROM OUR SIDE--BUT BY USING MY RING AND BACKING IT WITH ALL MY WILL POWER--I CAN GET THROUGH FROM THIS SIDE!

ND SHORTLY, IN A CERTAIN FAMILIAR UBICLE IN THE HANGAR OF THE ERRIS AIRCRAFT COMPANY, A OLEMN OATH IS RENEWED...
I HAD ONLY A FEW SECONDS OF POWER LEFT--
N BRIGHTEST DAY, IN BLACKEST NIGHT, NO EVIL SHALL ESCAPE MY SIGHT! ET THOSE WHO WORSHIP EVIL'S MIGHT BEWARE MY POWER--GREEN LANTERN'S LIGHT!

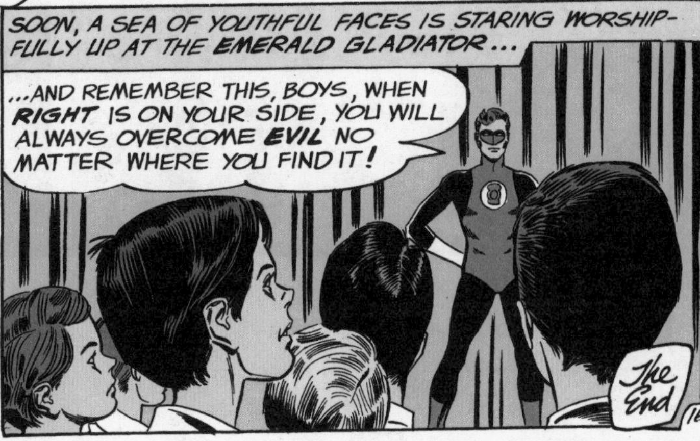
ON A ONCE-AGAIN PEACEFUL EARTH A BRILLIANT GREEN SHAPE FLARES ALONG...
THE OPENING OF THE BOYS SETTLEMENT HOUSE IN VALDALE HAS BEEN POST-PONED--DUE TO THE EXTRAORDINARY EVENTS YESTERDAY--TO TODAY! AND THIS TIME I'M KEEPING MY APPOINTMENT TO APPEAR THERE!
SOON, A SEA OF YOUTHFUL FACES IS STARING WORSHIP-FULLY UP AT THE EMERALD GLADIATOR...
...AND REMEMBER THIS, BOYS, WHEN RIGHT IS ON YOUR SIDE, YOU WILL ALWAYS OVERCOME EVIL NO MATTER WHERE YOU FIND IT!
The End
16

GREEN LANTERN

# SECRET ORIGIN OF THE GUARDIANS

**Writer:** JOHN BROOME **Penciller:** GIL KANE **Inker:** SID GREENE

Originally presented in GREEN LANTERN No. 40, October 1965

In 1964, John Broome and Gil Kane revealed the "Secret Origin" of the Guardians of the Universe in GREEN LANTERN #40. This beautifully illustrated tale delved into the beginnings of the immortals that created and oversaw the Green Lantern Corps. It also introduced the spark of a concept that Marv Wolfman and George Perez would later use as the basis of their entire landmark miniseries CRISIS ON INFINITE EARTHS. If you're a DC reader already, you'll probably recognize the scene as the Guardian Krona attempts to learn the secret of all creation by gazing back in time to the beginning of existence.

This story also features the first true team-up between Hal Jordan and the Golden Age Green Lantern, Alan Scott. Alan Scott was the lead character in the first volume of GREEN LANTERN comic books introduced in the 1940s. Unlike Hal Jordan, his ring was supernatural in nature and he wasn't connected to any Corps of any kind.

The Guardians of the Universe are an essential element to the Green Lantern Corps. Their origin reveals that even these immortals have their flaws and can make mistakes. The Guardians are mysterious, unpredictable and powerful on a level we haven't even begun to reveal, I think. But like all leaders, they can be in that position so long they can lose perspective. The current fractures among the Guardians that occurred in SINESTRO CORPS which sent two Guardians, Ganthet and Sayd, off to form their own Corps was a continued extension of the philosophical difference that had begun to be explored within this story.

Alan Scott, the Golden Age Green Lantern, is currently a main member of the Justice Society of America. He's a character that is connected to Hal Jordan and the Green Lantern Corps in name and spirit. He may not be an official officer of the Green Lantern Corps, but he's been an important part of their adventures for the last few decades. Additionally, it was later revealed that the supernatural source of Alan's power, the Starheart, was connected to the green power that fueled the rings of the Green Lantern Corps.

Look for that image of the massive hand coalescing stars and planets within its palm. It would become one of the most iconic images of the DC Universe during a Crisis.

– Geoff Johns

# GREEN LANTERN

CO-STARRING the "ORIGINAL" GREEN LANTERN IN A FULL-LENGTH POWER-PACKED NOVEL!

OLD THE TRUMP CARD IN THIS TTLE WITH MY RIVAL **GREEN NTERN!** I CAN SAFEGUARD SELF WITH THIS **YELLOW** IELD FROM THE EFFECTS OF S **POWER RING**--WHILE HE S **NOTHING** TO PROTECT M FROM THE POWER OF **MY RING!**

THE UNIVERSE IS DOOMED UNLESS OUR **HAL JORDAN — GREEN LANTERN** CAN DEFEAT THE **ALAN SCOTT — GREEN LANTERN** FROM ANOTHER EARTH!

YES! THE VERY EXISTENCE OF OUR UNIVERSE ITSELF HUNG IN THE BALANCE AS TWO **GREEN-CLAD CRUSADERS--HAL JORDAN** AND **ALAN SCOTT** (THE **GREEN LANTERN** OF **EARTH-TWO** AND OF ANOTHER, BYGONE ERA!) DUELLED WITH MIGHTY **POWER RINGS** IN A TITANIC BATTLE FROM WHICH ONLY **ONE** COULD EMERGE THE VICTOR! WHAT LAY BEHIND THIS SHOCKING, STARTLING COMBAT BETWEEN JUSTICE-LOVING RING-WEARERS? HOW DID IT ALL TIE IN WITH A FORBIDDEN EXPERIMENT TO SOLVE THE RIDDLE OF THE...

# SECRET ORIGIN OF THE GUARDIANS!

Story by John Broome
Art by Gil Kane & Sid Greene

AT A "COME AS YOU WERE" PARTY GIVEN BY THE GOTHAM BROADCASTING COMPANY ON EARTH-TWO*..
...THAT'S ALAN SCOTT! HE'S NOW THE PRESIDENT OF GOTHAM BROAD-CASTING! BUT TWENTY YEARS AGO HE WAS A RADIO ANNOUNCER... SO FOR THE PARTY HE'S PLAYING THAT ROLE AGAIN!
WHAT A FORCEFUL-LOOKING MAN! YOU CAN TELL HE WAS BOUND TO REACH THE TOP!
*EDITOR'S NOTE: EARTH-TWO IS A CONVENIENT DESIGNATION FOR A PARALLEL EARTH IN ANOTHER DIMENSION--WHERE LIFE, CUSTOMS, LANGUAGES--EVEN SUPER-HEROES--EVOLVED SIMILARLY TO THOSE ON EARTH-ONE!
AND THERE'S DOIBY DICKLES! HE'S MR. SCOTT'S MAN FRIDAY NOW! HE USED TO BE A CAB DRIVER--AND TO FIT IN WITH THE NOSTALGIC SPIRIT OF THE OCCASION, HE TOOK MR. SCOTT HERE IN HIS FAMOUS TAXI CALLED GOITRUDE!
HOW CUTE!
AS THE PARTY BREAKS UP...
GOITRUDE AWAITS YOUSE--WIT' "SOIVICE DAT DON'T MAKE YOUSE NOIVICE"!
HOW SWELL TO HEAR THAT OLD SLOGAN OF YOURS AGAIN, DOIBY!
IT WAS A GREAT IDEA--RELIVING OUR ROLES OF TWENTY YEARS AGO, eh, DOIBY?
AH--DEM WAS DA GOOD OLD DAYS, ALAN! YES SIRREE!
THEN, AS NOSTALGIC REMINISCENCES ARE RUDELY INTERRUPTED...
...AND WHAT LOOKS LIKE A SIZEABLE METEOR HAS BEEN SIGHTED OUT IN SPACE... HEADING DIRECTLY FOR GOTHAM CITY! WARNING...
A DANGEROUS METEOR! WHATCHA WAITIN' FER, PAL?
I GET THE MESSAGE, DOIBY!
2

IN THE BACK OF "GOITRUDE" A SWIFT TRANSFORMATION TAKES PLACE...
HURRY, LANTRIN! I T'INK I SEE IT COMIN' DIS WAY!
I'M ALL SET TO GO!

OUT OF THE STILL-ROLLING CAB CATAPULTS A UNIFORMED FIGURE THAT HAS THRILLED MANY A HEART...
THERE IT IS-- STREAKING IN VERY LOW! GOT TO BEAM MY RING ON IT BEFORE IT STRIKES--!
TAXI
I'LL CATCH UP TO YOUSE, GL--IN CASE MY VALUABLE ASSISTRANCE IS NEEDED!

UNERRINGLY, THE OCCULT POWER BEAM MEETS ITS TARGET! BUT STRANGELY ENOUGH...
IT BLASTED RIGHT THROUGH MY BEAM AND VANISHED!

IN FACT, THE ONLY CRASHING SOUND TO BE HEARD IS...
eh? DOIBY MUST HAVE BEEN WATCHING ME-- AND NOT WHERE HE WAS GOING! HE'S SMACKED INTO A TREE--!
CRASH!

IT MUST HAVE BEEN ROTTEN! HE'S CRACKED IT--GOING TO FALL ON HIM!
YOICKS! GOITRUDE'S IN DANGER! DAT TREE--! HELP, LANTRIN!
CRAACK!
3

INSTANTLY, THE GREEN-CLAD CRUSADER RESPONDS TO THE APPEAL...
MY POWER BEAM--THE TREE WAS DEFLECTED BY IT!
DOIBY, LOOK AT THAT!
TAXI
HUH? LOOK AT WOT--?

THE TREE WAS DEFLECTED BY MY RING! DIDN'T YOU SEE IT?
IMPOSSIBLE, LANTRIN! YER POWER BEAM HAS NO EFFECT ON ANY-THING MADE O' WOOD -- AND DAT'S A FACK!

ON IMPULSE, GREEN LANTERN TRIES OUT HIS BEAM ON THE TREE ONCE AGAIN..
NO EFFECT, eh? WHAT DO YOU CALL THAT?
IT'S A COCKEYED WONDER, DAT'S WOT IT IS! I DON'T UNDER-STAND!

YOU KNOW WHAT I THINK, DOIBY? IT HAD SOMETHING TO DO WITH THAT METEOR! SOMEHOW, CONTACT WITH THAT METEOR HAS ELIMINATED THE WEAKNESS OF MY RING! IT HAS NO WEAK-NESS ANYMORE! THIS IS TOO GOOD TO KEEP TO OURSELVES--

*EDITOR'S NOTE: DUE TO NECESSARY IMPURITIES IN THE POWER BATTERY, THE EARTH-ONE POWER RING CANNOT AFFECT ANYTHING COLORED YELLOW!

GEE, DAT'S MIGHTY BIG OF YOUSE TO T'INK RIGHT AWAY OF HELPIN' YER FRIEND, DA OTHER GREEN LANTRIN!
I'M TAKING RIGHT OFF, DOIBY! SEE YOU LATER!

SOON, THE WONDER BEAM IS CLEAVING THE VIBRATORY BARRIER BETWEEN THE TWO EARTHS...
I ALWAYS GET A KICK OUT OF VISITING HAL JORDAN, MY COUNTERPART GREEN LANTERN ON EARTH-ONE! BUT ESPECIALLY NOW WHEN I HAVE EXCITING NEWS TO TELL HIM!

IN DUE COURSE, AT THE FERRIS AIRCRAFT COMPANY WHERE TEST PILOT HAL JORDAN IS AT WORK...
I'M GETTING A MENTAL MESSAGE--FROM GREEN LANTERN OF EARTH-TWO! HE'S ARRIVED HERE ON OUR EARTH--AND IS WAITING TO SEE ME JUST OUTSIDE THE COMPANY AREA!

IN A CORNER OF THE HANGAR, A SWIFT CHANGE TAKES PLACE--AND A SOLEMN OATH IS RENEWED...
IN BRIGHTEST DAY, IN BLACKEST NIGHT, NO EVIL SHALL ESCAPE MY SIGHT! LET THOSE WHO WORSHIP EVIL'S MIGHT BEWARE MY POWER-- GREEN LANTERN'S LIGHT!

SHORTLY, NEARBY, A WARM REUNION...
GOOD TO SEE YOU AGAIN, ALAN!
FINE TO SEE YOU, HAL! WAIT TILL YOU HEAR THE EXCITING NEWS THAT BROUGHT ME HERE!

...AND AS A RESULT OF THAT METEOR, MY RING NOW HAS POWER OVER WOOD! WATCH--I'LL RAISE THAT WOODEN CRATE--
FERRIS AIRCR
5

BUT THEN, ASTONISHINGLY...
I--I DON'T UNDERSTAND! I--I CAN'T BUDGE THE CRATE--CAN'T AFFECT IT AT ALL! LOOKS LIKE I'VE MADE SOME KIND OF MISTAKE, HAL...!

I WAS SURE MY RING HAD POWER OVER WOOD--BUT OBVIOUSLY IT DOESN'T HAVE--ANY LONGER! SO MY VISIT HERE TO TRY AND HELP YOU WAS USELESS! I MIGHT AS WELL GET ON HOME--
NO, WAIT, ALAN! YOUR STORY HAS INTRIGUED ME...

AS EARTH-ONE'S GREEN GLADIATOR REFLECTS THOUGHTFULLY...
...A METEOR THAT COMES IN LOW...AT AN ODD ANGLE! THEN IT SEEMS TO SHOOT RIGHT THROUGH YOUR POWER BEAM AND DISAPPEAR...! AND AFTER THAT... YOUR RING SUDDENLY HAS POWER OVER WOOD...WHICH NOW JUST AS SUDDENLY DOESN'T HAVE ANYMORE! THIS IS A BIT OF A MYSTERY!

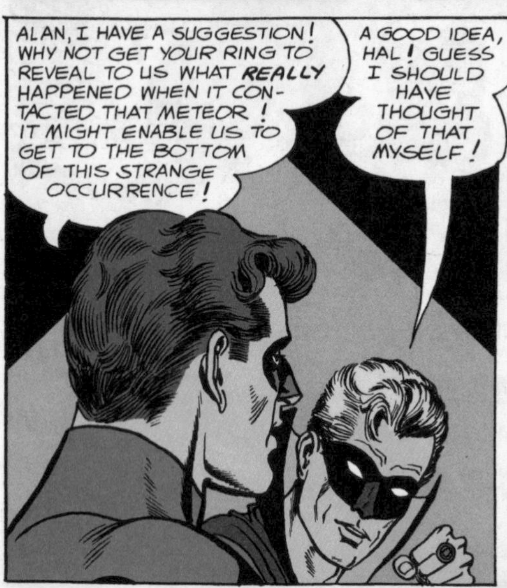
ALAN, I HAVE A SUGGESTION! WHY NOT GET YOUR RING TO REVEAL TO US WHAT REALLY HAPPENED WHEN IT CONTACTED THAT METEOR! IT MIGHT ENABLE US TO GET TO THE BOTTOM OF THIS STRANGE OCCURRENCE!
A GOOD IDEA, HAL! GUESS I SHOULD HAVE THOUGHT OF THAT MYSELF!

UNDER A MENTAL COMMAND, THE MYSTIC RING RESPONDS INSTANTLY...
TELL US WHAT REALLY HAPPENED WHEN I TRIED TO STOP THAT METEOR! LEAVE NO DETAILS OUT...!
TO BEGIN WITH... IT WAS NOT A METEOR...

"IT WAS REALLY A PACKET OF PURE ENERGY... THAT HAD BEEN CREATED TEN BILLION YEARS BEFORE! I KNOW THIS BECAUSE MY BEAM..."

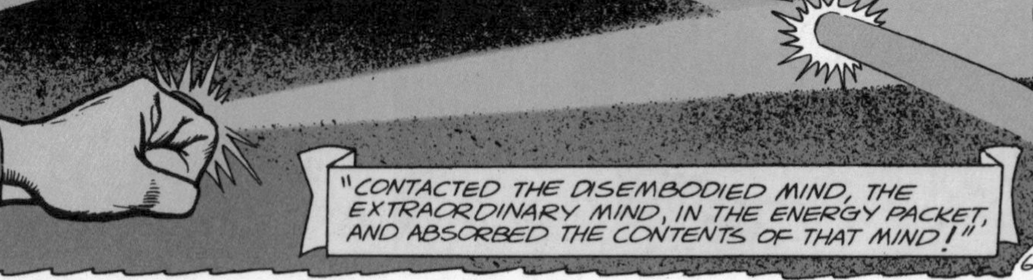
"CONTACTED THE DISEMBODIED MIND, THE EXTRAORDINARY MIND, IN THE ENERGY PACKET, AND ABSORBED THE CONTENTS OF THAT MIND!"
6

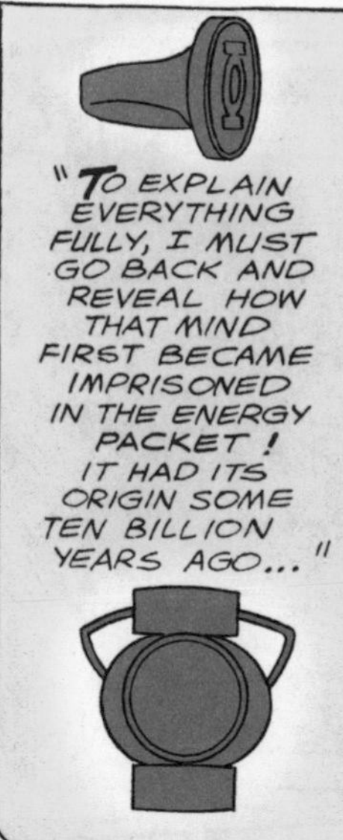
"TO EXPLAIN EVERYTHING FULLY, I MUST GO BACK AND REVEAL HOW THAT MIND FIRST BECAME IMPRISONED IN THE ENERGY PACKET! IT HAD ITS ORIGIN SOME TEN BILLION YEARS AGO..."

"AT WHICH TIME THERE DWELT ON THIS WORLD A RACE DIFFERENT FROM HUMANS WHO CALLED THEMSELVES OANS. THEY WERE IMMORTAL, NEVER NEEDED SLEEP OR REST..."
"THEY STRODE THE PLANET LIKE GIANTS..."

"THEIR TREMENDOUS NATURAL POWERS THEY EVINCED OFTEN AT THE EARLIEST AGE..."
LOOK! MY CHILD CAN ALREADY LIFT A GREAT BOULDER BY MENTAL FORCE!
VERY GOOD INDEED! MY SON COULD NOT DO THAT UNTIL HE WAS TWICE AS OLD!

"THE ADULTS AMONG THE OANS BUSIED THEMSELVES IN AN ETERNAL STUDY OF NATURE..."
WE STILL DO NOT KNOW THE TRUE ESSENCE OF LIGHT! BUT SINCE WE ARE IMMORTAL, WE HAVE ENDLESS TIME TO EXAMINE THE PROBLEM AND ONE DAY PERHAPS WE SHALL SOLVE IT...

"GAMES AND SPORTS ROUNDED OUT THEIR DAY! TRULY IT WAS A KIND OF PARADISE THEY LIVED IN..."
"BUT THERE WAS ONE DISTURBING NOTE IN THIS HARMONY, THAT TROUBLED THE OAN ELDERS..."

AMONG THEIR NUMBER WAS ONE NAMED KRONA WHOSE THOUGHTS WERE PRIMARILY CONCERNED WITH ONE THING ..."
BY THIS INSTRUMENT OF MY OWN DEVISING I SHALL PROBE THE BEGINNING OF ALL THINGS! NOTHING SHALL BE HIDDEN FROM ME!
KRONA, THERE IS A LEGEND OF TIME-LESS AGE AMONG US...

...THAT IF WE EVER LEARNED THE TRUTH ABOUT OUR SECRET ORIGINS, WE AND OUR UNIVERSE WOULD BE INSTANTLY DESTROYED!
BAH! SUCH LEGENDS ARE TALES ONLY FOOLS WOULD FEAR!

"DESPITE ALL PLEAS AND URGING, KRONA CONTINUED HIS CEASELESS LABORS, AND ONE DAY..."
AN IMAGE FORMING--!? A SHADOW LIKE A GIANT HAND... WITH SOMETHING... A CLUSTER OF STARS IN IT--! I MUST GO BACK FURTHER-- FURTHER--!
"THEN..."
YAAH--!
CKRACK
"THE TERRIBLE COSMIC LIGHTNING BOLT SPLINTERED THE MACHINE! IT WOULD HAVE DE-STROYED KRONA TOO HAD HE NOT BEEN IMMORTAL!"
"BUT FROM THAT MOMENT ON, EVIL WAS LOOSED ON THE UNIVERSE! IT SWIFTLY SPREAD FROM WORLD TO WORLD WHERE INTELLIGENT CREATURES LIVED WHO HAD NOT THE GIFT OF IMMORTALITY LIKE THE OANS..."
KILL... KILL!
"BROTHER KILLED BROTHER! HATRED AND VIOLENCE GREW, FLOURISHED! AND THE OANS, BY THEIR SUPER-MENTALITY, KNEW IT HAD ALL BEEN CAUSED BY KRONA'S INSATIABLE AMBITION!"
8

"ONCE AGAIN THEY WENT TO HIM AND APPEALED TO HIM-- AND ONCE AGAIN HE SPURNED THEM..."
I WILL NEVER CEASE SEARCHING TO LEARN OUR ORIGINS! YOU CANNOT PUNISH ME! I AM IMMORTAL!
THERE ARE WAYS TO STOP YOU, KRONA!

"WITH THEIR UNLIMITED POWERS, THEY SEIZED KRONA AND REDUCED HIM TO A DISEMBODIED STATE IN A PRISON OF ENERGY..."
THROUGH END-LESS TIME KRONA WILL CIRCLE THROUGH ALL UNIVERSES!
NEVER MORE WILL HIS AMBITION PLAGUE US!

"THEY THEN SET ABOUT TRYING TO STEM THE TIDE OF EVIL UNLEASHED BY THEIR AMBITIOUS FELLOW-OAN..."
WE SHALL BECOME THE GUARDIANS OF OUR UNIVERSE! WHEREVER WICKEDNESS RISES, WE WILL COMBAT IT--AND PROTECT JUSTICE!

"TO AID THEM, THEY CREATED ASSISTANTS CALLED GREEN LANTERNS IN VARIOUS SECTORS OF SPACE..."
KI-NILG, HERE IS YOUR POWER BATTERY... AND YOUR POWER RING! USE THEM WELL...

"ALSO THEY TOOK CARE OF ONE OTHER MATTER AT THIS PERIOD..."
THIS RADIATION WILL ENSURE THAT NONE OF US--AND NO POWER RING FORCE THAT STEMS FROM US--WILL EVER BE ABLE, AS KRONA TRIED, TO LEARN THE DREAD SECRET OF OUR ORIGINS! IT MUST REMAIN FOREVER HIDDEN!
9

"AS THE EONS PASSED, THE **OANS** EVOLVED, AS A FORM OF AGING, INTO THE **GUARDIANS** AS YOU KNOW THEM NOW..."

"STILL BATTLING EVIL AND AIDING ALL CREATURES OF GOOD WILL!"

"LONG BEFORE, THEY HAD FORGOTTEN **KRONA** TRAVELING THROUGH ENDLESS UNIVERSES IN HIS ENERGY-PRISON..."

"BUT **KRONA**, STILL ALIVE AND STILL POSSESSED OF HIS TREMENDOUS **MIND**, HAD NEVER GIVEN UP SCHEMING TO FREE HIMSELF!"

"RECENTLY TRAVERSING THE UNIVERSE OF **EARTH-TWO**, HIS RESTLESS DIABOLIC MENTALITY DETECTED THE LONG HOPED-FOR OPPORTUNITY..."
ON THIS APPROACHING PLANET... A CRUSADER CALLED **GREEN LANTERN** WITH A **POWER RING** FILLED WITH **OCCULT ENERGY**! IT IS POSSIBLE... THERE IS A CHANCE... THAT I CAN MAKE USE OF HIM TO GAIN MY FREEDOM...
"BY SHEER MIND-FORCE, **KRONA** INCREASED THE HEAT IN THE ENERGY-PACKET UNTIL IT GLOWED LIKE A METEOR..."
WARNING! A METEOR FALLING FROM SPACE! IT WILL LAND IN **GOTHAM CITY**! WARNING!
MY SCHEME IS WORKING--!

"YOU, TOO, BELIEVED IT WAS A METEOR! YOU FLARED OUT MY BEAM TO STOP IT, TO PRE-VENT DAMAGE..."
"BUT WHAT YOU DIDN'T REALIZE WAS THAT AT THE MOMENT OF CONTACT..."

"...THE BODILESS IMMORTAL MIND OF **KRONA**-- BY A PRODIGIOUS FEAT OF THE WILL-- STRUGGLED FREE OF THE ENERGY-PACKET AND PASSED DOWN MY MYSTIC BEAM..."
AFTER TEN BILLION YEARS-- **FREE!!**

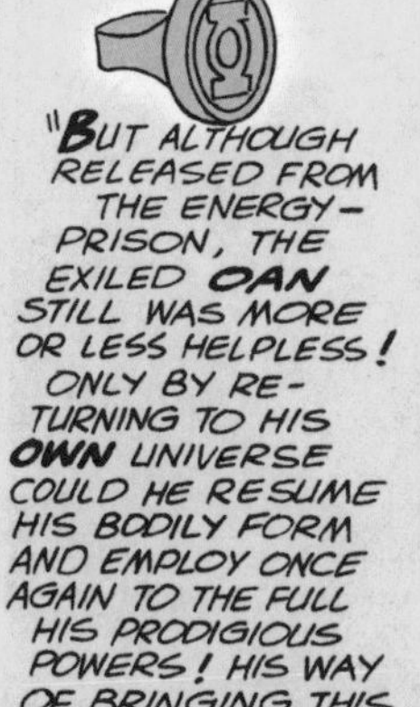
"BUT ALTHOUGH RELEASED FROM THE ENERGY-PRISON, THE EXILED OAN STILL WAS MORE OR LESS HELPLESS! ONLY BY RE-TURNING TO HIS OWN UNIVERSE COULD HE RESUME HIS BODILY FORM AND EMPLOY ONCE AGAIN TO THE FULL HIS PRODIGIOUS POWERS! HIS WAY OF BRINGING THIS ALL ABOUT..."

"...WAS TO ENABLE YOU, ALAN SCOTT, TEMPORARILY TO HAVE CONTROL OVER WOODEN OBJECTS!"
MY RING--LIFTING THIS WOODEN FENCE--!
"HE ANTICIPATED THAT YOU WOULD IMMEDIATELY THINK OF HELPING YOUR FRIEND, THE GREEN LANTERN OF EARTH-ONE.."

"SURE ENOUGH, YOU SPED HERE INTO KRONA'S UNIVERSE! BUT WHAT YOU DIDN'T REALIZE, AS YOU ARRIVED..."
NOW THAT I AM BACK IN MY OWN UNIVERSE, WHERE I...
...HAVE REGAINED MY FULL POWERS...
...I CAN DETACH MYSELF FROM THIS OCCULT RING... AND BECOME KRONA AGAIN!

"I THEREUPON LOST CONTACT WITH HIM AND CAN GIVE NO MORE INFORMATION..."
ALAN, THE FIRST THING I MUST DO IS NOTIFY THE GUARDIANS--WARN THEM OF WHAT HAS HAPPENED! AFTER THAT I MUST FIND KRONA!
WE MUST FIND KRONA! AFTER ALL, I'M RE-SPONSIBLE FOR HIS BEING HERE!
SOON, IN THE HANGAR DRESSING ROOM WHERE SECRETLY THE POWER BATTERY IS KEPT...
I'VE CON-TACTED THE GUARDIANS--eh?
YES! WE ALREADY KNOW WHAT YOU WANT TO TELL US, GREEN LANTERN! WE TOO LISTENED IN ON THE ACCOUNT OF YOUR FRIEND'S RING! THE SITUATION IS GRAVE! IT REQUIRES EMERGENCY ACTION!
11

KRONA IS SOMEWHERE ON EARTH! BUT HE HAS SET UP MENTAL DEFENSES TO PREVENT OUR DISCOVERING HIS EXACT LOCATION! UNDOUBTEDLY HE WILL SEEK AGAIN TO PROBE THE FORBIDDEN SECRET OF OUR ORIGINS! THIS COULD RESULT...

...IN THE INSTANTANEOUS DESTRUCTION OF THE UNIVERSE! OUR CALCULATIONS SHOW THAT THE FIRST RESULTS OF HIS MAD EFFORTS WILL BE A TERRIBLE OUTPOURING OF EVIL IN HIS IMMEDIATE VICINITY! THAT MEANS...

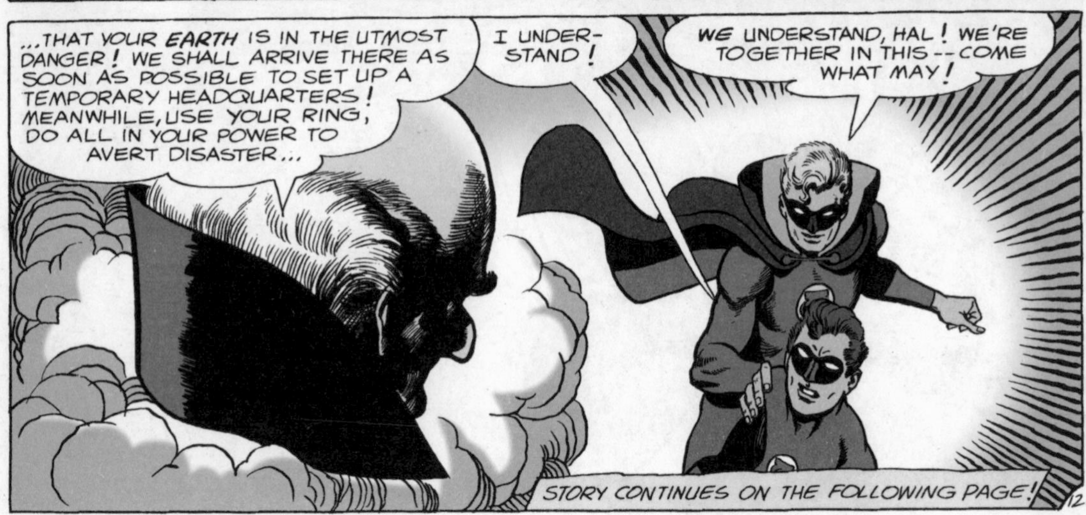
...THAT YOUR EARTH IS IN THE UTMOST DANGER! WE SHALL ARRIVE THERE AS SOON AS POSSIBLE TO SET UP A TEMPORARY HEADQUARTERS! MEANWHILE, USE YOUR RING, DO ALL IN YOUR POWER TO AVERT DISASTER...
I UNDERSTAND!
WE UNDERSTAND, HAL! WE'RE TOGETHER IN THIS--COME WHAT MAY!
STORY CONTINUES ON THE FOLLOWING PAGE!
12

GREEN LANTERN

SECRET ORIGIN of the GUARDIANS!--PART 2
WRACKED BY INVISIBLE WAVES OF EVIL SPREADING FROM KRONA'S PRESENCE ON EARTH-ONE, THE PLANET ITSELF GOES BERSERK, SEEKING IN FURY AND HATRED TO DESTROY THE HUMANITY THAT HAS SPAWNED ON ITS SURFACE!
NEAR COAST CITY, MIGHTY COAST RIVER RISES UP FROM ITS BANKS, INSANELY, WITH MURDEROUS INTENT, STRIKING TO BOTH SIDES OF ITS GREAT CHANNEL! AND WHILE ALL OVER THE UNIVERSE, ON MANY WORLDS, DIFFERENT GREEN LANTERNS ARE STRAINING TO COMBAT THE UPSURGE OF EVIL, HERE ON EARTH-TWO, A DUO OF GREEN LANTERNS SPEEDS TO MEET THE GREATEST AND MOST INTENSE THREAT OF ALL...
THANKS TO THE GUARDIANS, THE ALERT IS ON, HAL! THAT RIVER IS RUNNING AMOK! CHURNING OVER ITS BANKS LIKE A WILD BEAST!
YOU TAKE THE LEFT SIDE, ALAN--I'LL TAKE THE RIGHT! GOT TO PROTECT THOSE PEOPLE FROM HARM!
13

AT ONCE THE VISITING **GREEN LANTERN** OF **EARTH-TWO** BURSTS INTO ACTION, TRAINING HIS MIGHTY RING AT THE RAGING WATERS...
WAVES LIKE ENORMOUS PINCERS--TRYING TO CRUSH THOSE PEOPLE! BUT MY BEAM HAS FROZEN THE WATER INTO SOLID ICE--STOPPED IT **COLD!**

WHILE ON THE OTHER SIDE OF THE RIVER...
MY RING IS CREATING HUGE ATOMIC OVENS INSIDE THE WAVES--TURNING THE WATER INTO STEAM--AS FAST AS IT COMES UP FROM ITS BED! THOSE PEOPLE ARE SAFE FOR THE TIME BEING--!

AND SOON AFTER, ANOTHER DREAD SPECTACLE ENGAGES THE TWIN RING-WIELDERS! FOR **MOUNT PACIFIC**, TOWERING OVER **COAST CITY**, HAS THRUST A HUGE TONGUE OF ITSELF UPWARD--LIKE THE TONGUE OF A HUGE SLAVERING WOLF!--AND A WEIGHT OF MILLIONS OF TONS OF EARTH WHIRLS TOWARD THE HELPLESS METROPOLIS--!

THE MOUNTAIN IS BENDING OVER--LIKE SOMETHING **ALIVE!** HURTLING TOWARD THE CITY!

IT'S SPROUTED LIKE A GIGANTIC ONION--AND THE TOP PART ELONGATED--WHIRLING--LIKE A HUGE WHIP--TOWARD THOSE BUILDINGS! AT IT, ALAN, WITH FULL POWER!

14

AS TWIN GREEN BEAMS SWIFTLY FORM COLOSSAL IMPLEMENTS TO ATTACK THE HUGE "WHIP" AND HALT ITS MAD THRUST AT HUMANITY...
ALAN HAS FORMED AN ENORMOUS **SAW** WITH HIS RING--SLICING THROUGH THE MENACE--!
HAL'S BEAM HAS CREATED A MAMMOTH RIVETING MACHINE--JOLTING THE "TONGUE" TO PIECES--!

DEFEATED, THE MOUNTAIN SEEMS TO WITHDRAW INTO ITSELF, AS IF TO LICK ITS WOUNDS...

WE BEAT IT! THE MOUNTAIN IS SHRINKING BACK--!

***MOTHER NATURE'S*** NOT CALLING IT QUITS YET, ALAN! LOOK--THAT ***CLOUD!***

ANGRY CLOUDS, FLOATING TOGETHER, HAVE FORMED AN AERIAL WHIRLPOOL, REVOLVING AT INCREDIBLE SPEED...

THE TORNADO-LIKE CLOUD--WHIPPING UP TERRIFIC WINDS!

IF IT STRIKES THE CITY, IT WILL LEVEL IT IN MOMENTS--!

INSTANTLY, THE GREEN-CLAD SENTINELS ARE ON THE MOVE, SEEDING THE WHIRLING CLOUD WITH ***SILVER IODIDE*** CRYSTALS FORMED BY THEIR REMARKABLE RINGS...

THE CLOUD MATTER IS CONDENSING AROUND THE SILVER IODIDE CRYSTALS CREATED BY OUR BEAMS AND TURNING INTO ***RAIN!***

THE RAIN IS FALLING IN TORRENTS--BUT AT LEAST IT WON'T HARM ANYONE THIS WAY!

15

THEN, SUDDENLY...
ALAN! ONE OF THE GUARDIANS -- APPEARING BEFORE US!
PAY HEED! WE HAVE ARRIVED ON THIS PLANET AND HAVE SET UP A TEMPORARY HEADQUARTERS! YOU MUST JOIN US AT ONCE--TO PLAN OUR BATTLE AGAINST KRONA!

YOU NEED NO LONGER FEAR THE OUTPOURING OF EVIL! OUR PRES-ENCES HERE ARE ENOUGH TO HOLD IN CHECK THE WAVES OF EVIL CAUSED BY KRONA! FOLLOW MY IMAGE--IT WILL LEAD YOU TO US!

SOON, AN UNEXPECTED DEVELOPMENT AT THE GUARDIANS' TEMPORARY HEADQUARTERS, AN UNUSED COURTROOM IN COAST CITY...
TURN IN YOUR POWER RING AND UNIFORM, HAL JORDAN! ALAN SCOTT IS REPLACING YOU AS GREEN LANTERN OF EARTH!
WHAT?!

I'VE DONE EVERYTHING YOU'VE EVER ASKED ME! I'VE NEVER SHIRKED A DUTY! I'VE SUFFERED AND FOUGHT--AND NOW YOU SUDDENLY TAKE AWAY MY STATUS AS GREEN LANTERN--AND GIVE IT TO ALAN SCOTT? WHY? WHY? WHY?
STORY CONTINUES ON THE FOLLOWING PAGE!
16

GREEN LANTERN

# SECRET ORIGIN of the GUARDIANS! --PART 3

HAL JORDAN DISPOSED AS **GREEN LANTERN--!** WHAT COULD ACCOUNT FOR THIS SHOCKING SWITCH ON THE PART OF THE **GUARDIANS?** TO UNDERSTAND, LET US ONCE AGAIN TURN BACK THE CLOCK A SHORT WHILE--TO THE INCREDIBLE **KRONA**, BLACK SHEEP OF THE IMMORTAL **OAN** RACE, INTENT ON HIS REVENGE AGAINST HIS FELLOW **OANS**--NOW KNOWN AS THE **GUARDIANS**--IN A CAVE OUTSIDE **COAST CITY** WHERE HE HAS SET UP A FANTASTIC WORKSHOP...

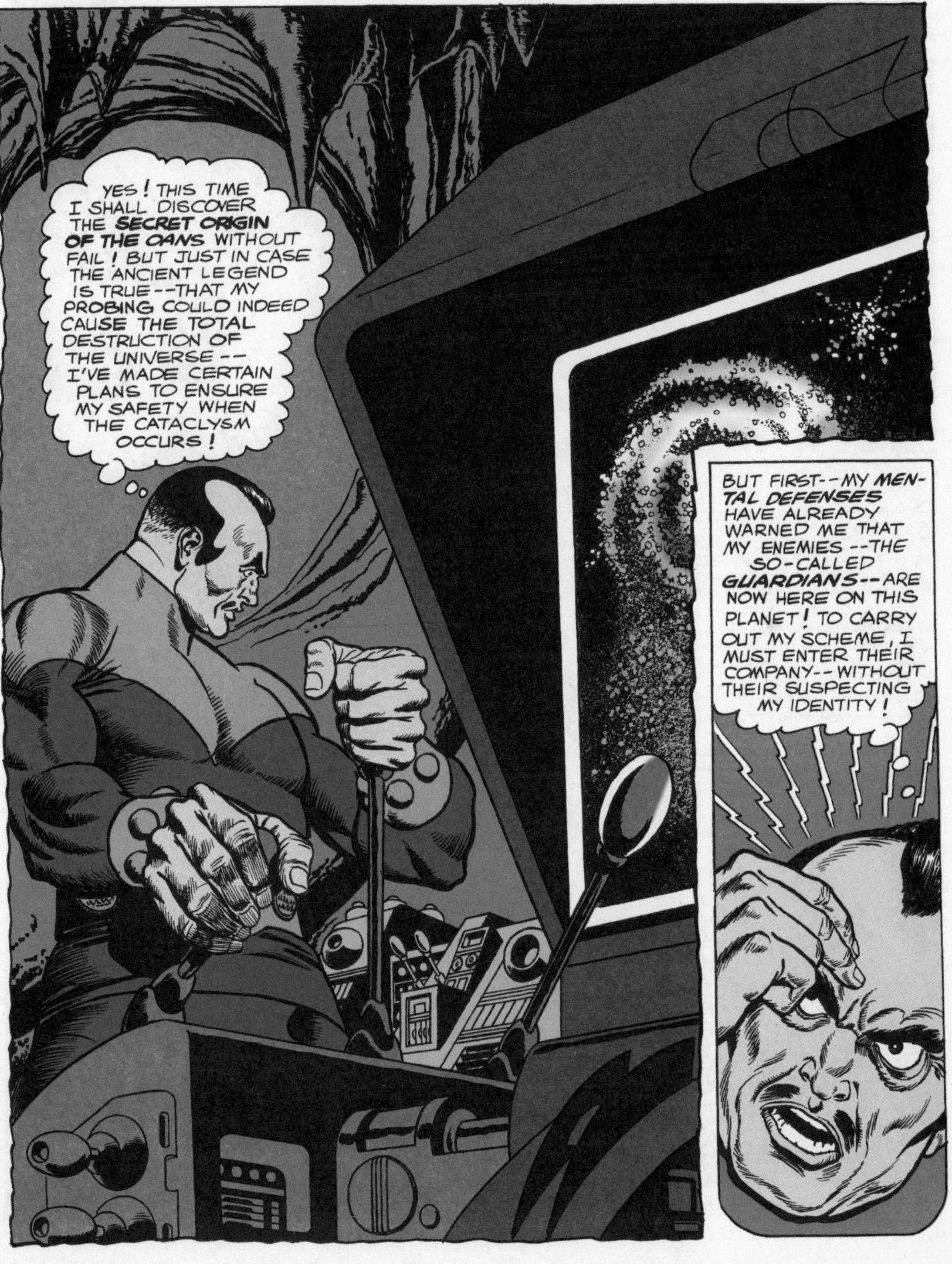

YES! THIS TIME I SHALL DISCOVER THE SECRET ORIGIN OF THE OANS WITHOUT FAIL! BUT JUST IN CASE THE ANCIENT LEGEND IS TRUE--THAT MY PROBING COULD INDEED CAUSE THE TOTAL DESTRUCTION OF THE UNIVERSE--I'VE MADE CERTAIN PLANS TO ENSURE MY SAFETY WHEN THE CATACLYSM OCCURS!
BUT FIRST--MY MENTAL DEFENSES HAVE ALREADY WARNED ME THAT MY ENEMIES--THE SO-CALLED GUARDIANS--ARE NOW HERE ON THIS PLANET! TO CARRY OUT MY SCHEME, I MUST ENTER THEIR COMPANY--WITHOUT THEIR SUSPECTING MY IDENTITY!

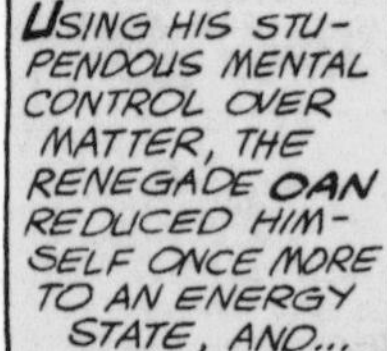
USING HIS STUPENDOUS MENTAL CONTROL OVER MATTER, THE RENEGADE OAN REDUCED HIMSELF ONCE MORE TO AN ENERGY STATE, AND...

IT WAS EASY ENOUGH TO LOCATE THESE TWO GREEN LANTERNS... BY TUNING IN ON THE SPECIAL VIBRATIONS GIVEN OFF BY THEIR POWER BEAMS!...

THEN, AT BLINDING SPEED, INVISIBLY, A STARTLING EVENT OCCURRED...
I'M TAKING OVER THE BODY OF THE ONE CALLED ALAN SCOTT! I HAVE URGENT NEED FOR HIS BODY!... AT THE SAME TIME I'M EJECTING HIS MIND-- FOR WHICH I HAVE NO NEED...!

THUS KRONA GAINED HIS INITIAL OBJECTIVE: CLOSE PROXIMITY TO THE GUARDIANS WITHOUT AROUSING THEIR SUSPICIONS...

FROM THIS SHORT DISTANCE... I'M ABLE TO CAST AN UNBREAKABLE SPELL OVER THE GUARDIANS! FROM NOW ON, THEY'LL DO WHAT I MENTALLY COMMAND THEM--!

THUS IT WAS UNDER THE EVIL OAN'S SINISTER INFLUENCE THAT THE PROTECTORS OF THE UNIVERSE ISSUED THEIR STARTLING ORDER...
TURN IN YOUR POWER RING AND UNIFORM, HAL JORDAN! ALAN SCOTT IS REPLACING YOU AS GREEN LANTERN OF EARTH!
WHAT?!
BUT NOW TO PICK UP OUR NARRATIVE AGAIN FROM THE POINT WHERE WE LEFT IT...

AS A STUNNED HAL JORDAN REACTS VIOLENTLY...
NOTHING DOING! THE ONLY WAY I'LL QUIT IS IF SCOTT CAN BEAT ME IN A GREEN LANTERN DUEL! AND I'M CHALLENGING HIM TO TAKE ME ON RIGHT NOW!
18

ON YOUR GUARD, GREEN LANTERN OF EARTH-TWO!
COMING AT ME FURIOUSLY--HIS RING BLAZING! TOO LATE NOW TO ATTEMPT MENTAL CONTROL OVER HIM! I'LL HAVE TO ACCEPT THE FOOL'S CHALLENGE! BUT I WON'T TAKE ANY RISKS--!

USING ALAN SCOTT'S RING, THE WILY KRONA SETS UP A YELLOW SHIELD THAT PROTECTS HIM FROM HIS RIVAL'S BEAM! AND AT THE SAME TIME...
THAT YELLOW SHIELD--MY RING CAN'T PENETRATE IT! UHHH--
CRASH!

AS THE DISGUISED OAN FOLLOWS UP HIS ADVANTAGE...
STILL IN ONE PIECE--?! HE HAS MORE ENDURANCE THAN I THOUGHT! BUT IT WON'T HELP HIM--
¡WHEW! ALAN SURE HAS A MAD ON--!

AGAIN THE MIGHTY BEAM, INCREASED BY KRONA'S MIND-FORCE, FLARES OUT...
AS THESE EARTHLINGS WOULD PUT IT--I'VE KNOCKED THE LIVING DAYLIGHTS OUT OF HIM!

I'D LIKE TO DESTROY HIM UTTERLY... BUT MY MIND-FORCE INFORMS ME IT WOULD BE EXTREMELY DIFFICULT--IF NOT IMPOSSIBLE! EVIDENTLY HIS RING AUTOMATICALLY ACTS TO PROTECT HIM IN CASE OF MORTAL DANGER! WELL, HE WON'T BOTHER ME ANYMORE! AND IN ANY EVENT...

...IF THIS ENTIRE UNIVERSE DISINTEGRATES DUE TO MY--er--EXPERIMENTS--HE'LL GO WITH IT! HIS RING WON'T SAVE HIM THEN!*
*EDITOR'S NOTE: TRUE! GREEN LANTERN'S RING WILL PROTECT HIM ONLY FROM DANGERS WITHIN THE UNIVERSE, NOT FROM THE DESTRUCTION OF THE UNIVERSE ITSELF!
19

AND SOON, IN THE CAVE OUTSIDE COAST CITY WHERE THE EVIL OAN HAS TRANSPORTED HIS GUARDIAN CAPTIVES BY MIND-POWER...
WE KNOW NOW IT IS THE MIND OF KRONA THAT HAS US IN THRALL!
YES! BUT WE ARE HELPLESS TO BREAK LOOSE FROM THE EVIL SPELL HE MANAGED TO THROW OVER US WHILE IN DISGUISE--!
NOW, MY FELLOW OANS, YOU SHALL WITNESS MY ULTIMATE TRIUMPH..! NOT ONLY WILL I EXPOSE OUR SECRET ORIGIN-- BUT I SHALL DO IT RIGHT IN FRONT OF YOUR EYES!

THAT WAY, MY PLEASURE IN BREAKING THE ONE GREAT FORBIDDEN RULE OF OUR RACE WILL BE INFINITELY INCREASED--BY YOUR TERROR AND FEAR WHEN IT HAPPENS!

THEN...
BUT FIRST... TO RE-ENTER MY OWN BODY...
..THERE IS NO LONGER ANY REASON...
...FOR DIS-GUISING MYSELF!

BY MENTAL FORCE I HAVE CREATED A DUPLICATE OF ALAN SCOTT'S POWER RING! THIS IS OF VITAL IMPORTANCE IN MY PLANS! IT IS THE KEY DEVICE I MUST USE TO SPIRIT MYSELF AWAY FROM HARM--IN CASE OUR ANCIENT LEGEND REALLY COMES TRUE--AND THIS UNIVERSE STARTS TO DISINTEGRATE!

FOR YOU SEE, THIS POWER RING IS NOT OF THIS UNIVERSE--AND WILL NOT BE AFFECTED BY ITS COLLAPSE! IT WILL AUTOMATICALLY BEAR ME TO SAFETY--TO THE UNIVERSE OF EARTH-TWO! CUNNING--AM I NOT?
20

THEN, BEFORE THE HORRIFIED EYES OF THE GUARDIANS, POWERLESS TO MOVE... TO INTERFERE WITH THEIR EX-COLLEAGUE'S SINISTER PLAN...
THIS TIME NO COSMIC LIGHTNING BOLT WILL HALT MY ATTEMPT! I HAVE SHIELDED MY WORKSHOP HERE FROM ANY SUCH ACCIDENT!
THERE..! AGAIN...THE FORMLESS HAND-LIKE CLOUD... THE STARRY NEBULA!... BUT I MUST GO BACK FURTHER... TO THE BEGINNING... TO OUR VERY ORIGIN!...

MEANWHILE...
...HAL... WAKE UP... YOU MUST LISTEN TO ME...!
ALAN SCOTT... CONTACTING ME TELEPATHICALLY..!

QUESTINGLY, THE POWER BEAM FLARES OUT AND...
ALAN!
KRONA TOOK OVER MY BODY! AND HE'S TAKEN CONTROL OF THE GUARDIANS TOO! I'VE BEEN SEARCHING FOR YOU! LISTEN--THERE'S HARDLY ANY TIME LEFT--

AS THE BODILESS HERO REVEALS TO HIS COMRADE-IN-ARMS THE DUPLICITY OF KRONA AND ALL THAT HAS OCCURRED...
I KNOW ALL THIS, HAL, BECAUSE IN THIS DISEMBODIED STATE MY MIND HAS WIDE TELEPATHIC POWERS--! YOU MUST STOP KRONA!
ALAN'S WARNING-- GIVING ME STRENGTH TO CARRY ON THE FIGHT AGAINST KRONA! I SURE COULD USE HIS HELP!

SUMMONING UP ALL MY WILL POWER, ALAN--TO COMMAND MY RING TO ABSORB YOUR MIND INTO MY OWN BRAIN--! THAT WAY WE CAN BATTLE KRONA TOGETHER!
I'LL GUIDE YOU TO HIM!

AS THE DOUBLE-MINDED GREEN LANTERN FLIES OFF TO CONTACT KRONA...
FANTASTIC LIGHTNING--! THE SKY GROWING DARK--!
HURRY! DOOMSDAY IS ALMOST UPON US!
21

AS A TIMELY ARRIVAL INTERRUPTS THE EVIL OAN'S HOUR OF TRIUMPH...
IN ANOTHER MOMENT I'LL KNOW THE SECRET-- eh? THAT GREEN LANTERN AGAIN-- BLUNDERING IN ON ME!
AT HIM, HAL!
HERE GOES, ALAN--!

Bah! IT IS ALMOST TOO EASY TO DEFEAT HIM! A MERE MATTER OF INSTANTLY ERECTING A YELLOW BARRIER BEFORE ME--THAT HIS POWER BEAM CANNOT PIERCE--

--WHILE AT THE SAME INSTANT I SHOOT A BURST OF THIS RING'S OVERWHELMING POWER AT HIM--UH--
OUR PLAN'S WORKING!

TO HIS STUNNED AMAZEMENT, THINGS DON'T GO QUITE ACCORDING TO PLAN FOR KRONA...
WE'VE SENT HIM REELING! PRESS ON, HAL--DON'T GIVE HIM TIME TO RECOVER!
HOW CAN I MISS--WITH ALAN ROOTING ME ON!

BUT EVEN THOUGH STRICKEN, THE EVIL OAN IS STILL PLENTY DANGEROUS...
A COSMIC LIGHTNING BOLT WILL FLATTEN HIM--!
SOMETHING COMING FROM HIS MIND--WITH TREMENDOUS POWERS!
22

AGAIN THE GRIM GLADIATOR IS HURLED BACKWARD...
HAL! HAL!
RELAX, PAL--HE HASN'T WON YET! LISTEN--WHEN I GIVE THE SIGNAL--ADD YOUR WILL POWER TO MINE! GIVE IT ALL YOU'VE GOT!

THEN, AS THE STEEL-LIKE STRENGTH OF WILL OF BOTH HEROES COMBINES WITH SHATTERING EFFECT AGAINST THEIR FOE...
WE'VE KNOCKED HIM DOWN! WEAKENED HIM--DAZED HIM!
WHAM!

AT THAT INSTANT, WITH KRONA'S CONCENTRATION BROKEN, HIS OMNIPOTENT ENEMIES, THE GUARDIANS, BURST LOOSE FROM THRALL...
FIRST WE DESTROY THE DIABOLIC DEVICE THAT THREATENED OUR FORBIDDEN SECRET...
CRACK

THEN WE DEAL WITH YOU, KRONA--!
I'M WEAK... IN YOUR POWER... BUT I STILL DEFY YOU!
YOUR DEFIANCE CANNOT HELP YOU NOW!

SHORTLY...
WE HAVE ONCE AGAIN REDUCED KRONA TO AN ENERGY-FORM! BUT THIS TIME WE HAVE SENT HIM OFF ON AN ORBIT THAT WILL NEVER INTERSECT ANY PLANET OR STAR! NEVER AGAIN WILL HE BE ABLE TO FREE HIMSELF--OR THREATEN ANY UNIVERSE!
23

LATER, AFTER THE GUARDIANS HAVE RETURNED TO OA AND GREEN LANTERN'S RING HAS REPLACED ALAN SCOTT'S MIND IN HIS OWN BODY...
THE IDEA OF SWITCHING POWER RINGS--SO THAT I HAD ON THE RING FROM YOUR BODY INSTEAD OF MY OWN--WAS AN INSPIRATION, ALAN!
YES, IT GAVE US THE ADVANTAGE OF SURPRISE, HAL--WHEN MY RING'S BEAM PIERCED KRONA'S YELLOW ENERGY-SHIELD!

THAT TRICK SURE SAVED THE DAY! BUT--WHOSE IDEA WAS IT, YOURS OR MINE? YOU KNOW, I CAN'T RECALL--!
WHAT DIFFERENCE DOES IT MAKE? WE WERE BOTH IN THE SAME BRAIN!

SO I GUESS WE CAN BOTH TAKE THE CREDIT! AND NOW, I'VE GOT TO GET BACK TO MY OWN EARTH! SO LONG, HAL!
'BY, ALAN! THANKS--THANKS FOR THE TERRIFIC TEAMWORK!

AS A WEARY GREEN LANTERN OF EARTH DRAWS A DEEP BREATH...
THE SUN IS SHINING NOW--AND ALL IS PEACEFUL! HOW BEAUTIFUL EVERYTHING IS NOW THAT THE MENACE IS OVER! I CAN ONLY HOPE IT STAYS THAT WAY--AND THAT KRONA NEVER GETS LOOSE TO SPREAD EVIL AND TERROR AGAIN..!
The End
24

GREEN LANTERN

# EARTH'S OTHER GREEN LANTERN

**Writer:** JOHN BROOME **Penciller:** GIL KANE **Inker:** SID GREENE

Originally presented in GREEN LANTERN No. 59, March 1968

The following story, "Earth's Other Green Lantern," again written by John Broome and illustrated by Gil Kane, introduced Guy Gardner. Guy is introduced as Abin Sur's second choice, due strictly to the fact that he was farther away from the crash site than Hal Jordan was. The idea of being "second best" was subsequently branded on Guy Gardner by creators Steve Englehart and Joe Staton in GREEN LANTERN and later mastered by Keith Giffen, J.M. DeMatteis and Kevin Maguire in JUSTICE LEAGUE INTERNATIONAL. Due to his over-the-top testosterone and rough-and-tumble attitude, Guy became a fan favorite two decades after he first appeared. Later, Beau Smith delved even deeper into Guy Gardner in WARRIOR, showing us the true heart of a hero that was hidden behind his gruff exterior.

Guy Gardner lost his status as Green Lantern shortly before Hal Jordan lost his. When I began working on GREEN LANTERN: REBIRTH and the return of Hal Jordan, I immediately knew that the series wouldn't just be about the resurrection of Hal Jordan. Guy Gardner had a unique personality in the DC Universe. He had gone on and on about how he didn't "need" a power ring or "miss" being a Green Lantern. But I knew the truth. I knew deep down in there, Guy missed it. And deep down in there, what drives Guy to strive so hard is that he was chosen second. No matter what happens, no matter what he accomplishes from here on out, he was chosen second. And that bothers him more than anybody else.

Even today.

But he'll never admit it.

Guy Gardner is a vital character to the Green Lantern mythos and one that I absolutely love working with. He continues to have a starring role in GREEN LANTERN CORPS and will continue to be a prominent hero throughout GREEN LANTERN: THE BLACKEST NIGHT.

– Geoff Johns

MY NAME IS HAL JORDAN--BETTER KNOWN TO YOU AS...
GREEN LANTERN
NOW--TAKE A LOOK AT THE GUY BEHIND ME! HE'S WEARING MY UNIFORM--FIGHTING MY MOST FORMIDABLE FOES--WITH MY POWER RING!
AND YET, I MUST ADMIT, HE HAS JUST AS MUCH RIGHT TO THAT UNIFORM AS I HAVE! BECAUSE HE IS ...
"EARTH'S OTHER GREEN LANTERN!"
STORY BY: JOHN BROOME
ART BY: GIL KANE & SID GREENE

TRANSPORTED TO OA* FOR AN INTENSIVE TWO-DAY SEMINAR IN THE HIGHER TECHNIQUES OF THE GUARDIANS, HAL JORDAN, THE GREEN LANTERN OF EARTH, IS SHOWN MANY STARTLING WONDERS...

...AND WHEREAS ORDINARY TELESCOPES CAN OBSERVE SCENES ON FAR-DISTANT WORLDS ONLY AS THEY EXISTED YEARS AGO--

THIS ONE SEES WORLDLY EVENTS AS THEY OCCUR NOW!

THIS MACHINE IS A MEMORY BANK--BUT A VERY SPECIAL ONE! IT STORES DATA TAKEN FROM BRAINS AFTER DEATH!

AFTER--DEATH?!

*OA--HOME OF THE IMMORTAL GUARDIANS OF THE UNIVERSE!

IT IS ONE OF OUR PROUDEST ACHIEVEMENTS! WE CALL IT MENTAL POST-MORTEMS!

FOR EXAMPLE, YOU MAY NOT BE AWARE THAT WE TELEPORTED THE BODY OF YOUR PREDECESSOR, ABIN SUR, BACK HERE TO OA.

BEFORE HE WAS ENSHRINED IN THE CRYPT, WE RECORDED ABIN SUR'S LAST HOURS ON EARTH--TAKEN FROM HIS OWN BRAIN! WOULD YOU LIKE TO VIEW IT?

VERY MUCH!

AS A SLIM CARTRIDGE CLICKS INTO PLACE IN THE MACHINE...
I'VE ALWAYS BEEN CURIOUS ABOUT ABIN SUR-- WHO SELECTED ME AS GREEN LANTERN WHEN HE WAS DYING...
...AND WHEN I CAME TO AFTER CRASH-LANDING ON THE PLANET EARTH, I KNEW THAT THE WORST HAD HAPPENED...
THIS IS UNCANNY--LIKE LISTENING TO A VOICE FROM THE OTHER SIDE OF THE TOMB!

NO USE...FOOLING YOURSELF, ABIN SUR... YOU ARE DYING...
YOU HAVE ONLY A SHORT TIME LEFT TO LIVE...
2

IN THIS EMERGENCY, STRICKEN AS YOU ARE, YOU ARE UNABLE TO CONTACT THE GUARDIANS!
YOUR DUTY IS CLEAR--PASS ON THE BATTERY OF POWER... TO A DESERVING ONE!
YOU MUST QUICKLY FIND ON THIS PLANET A DE-SERVING EARTHMAN... PASS ON TO HIM THE BATTERY OF POWER..!
"I PRESSED MY POWER RING TO THE BATTERY BESIDE ME..."
BATTERY OF POWER... SEEK IN THIS WORLD... IF THERE BE A DESERVING ONE HERE! SEEK AND FIND... AND BRING HIM TO ME!
"FROM THE RING A BOLT OF PURE ENERGY CRISS-CROSSED THE PLANET WITH THE SPEED OF LIGHT... SEARCHING..."
HE MUST BE ONE WITHOUT FEAR! ENTIRELY WITHOUT FEAR! HURRY! THE TIME IS SHORT!
"IN HARDLY MORE THAN INSTANTS, THOUGHTS PULSED BACK TO ME..."
THERE ARE TWO DESERVING ONES!... ONE IS GUY GARDNER-- AN INSTRUCTOR IN AN EASTERN SCHOOL IN THIS COUNTRY!
THE OTHER IS A TEST-PILOT NAMED HAL JORDAN IN NEARBY CALIFORNIA! BOTH ARE IDENTICALLY WORTHY--AND FREE FROM FEAR!

TWO?! AND IDENTICALLY DESERVING--!?
IN THAT CASE--I'LL SELECT THE NEAREST ONE!
GO! BRING THE TEST-PILOT BACK HERE--SWIFTLY AS POSSIBLE!

THE BEAM DARTED OFF AGAIN...TO A CERTAIN AIRCRAFT HANGAR AT THE FERRIS AIRCRAFT COMPANY..."
THIS FLIGHTLESS TRAINER WILL HELP TURN OUT SPACE-PILOTS OF THE FUTURE--

"A GREEN GLOW SURROUNDED THE FLYER AND...
I'M SCOOTING OFF AT FANTASTIC SPEED--!
HOW COULD SUCH AN INCREDIBLE THING HAPPEN?

"AS THE FLIGHT ABRUPTLY ENDED..."
COME IN, HAL JORDAN!
GOOD GOSH!
A SPACEMAN--IN THIS WRECKED SPACE-SHIP--COMMUNICATING WITH ME BY TELEPATHY!

I AM ABIN SUR...OF A FAR-DISTANT WORLD...AND I AM DYING...
THERE IS NOTHING YOU CAN DO TO HELP ME...BESIDES, I MUST SPEAK TO YOU...OF A MORE IMPORTANT MATTER...
MORE IMPORTANT... THAN YOUR LIFE?

YES... LOOK AT THIS OBJECT, HAL JORDAN...
WHY...IT LOOKS LIKE A GREEN LANTERN...
4

YES... AND THOSE WHO POSSESS IT ARE KNOWN AS GREEN LANTERNS... BUT ACTUALLY IT IS A BATTERY OF POWER...
GIVEN ONLY TO SELECTED INDIVIDUALS ON SCATTERED WORLDS OF THE COSMOS... TO BE USED AS A WEAPON AGAINST FORCES OF EVIL AND INJUSTICE...
IT IS A GREEN LANTERN'S DUTY... WHEN DISASTER STRIKES... AS IT HAS STRUCK ME... TO PASS ON THE BATTERY OF POWER... TO ANOTHER WHO IS FEARLESS... AND HONEST! COME CLOSER TO ME...
YES... BY THE BEAM OF MY RING... I SEE THAT YOU ARE HONEST! AND THE BATTERY HAS ALREADY SELECTED YOU AS ONE BORN WITHOUT FEAR! SO YOU PASS BOTH TESTS, HAL JORDAN...
"THERE WAS STILL MUCH TO TELL HIM... AND ONLY MOMENTS REMAINING TO ME! I DESCRIBED HOW MY SHIP WAS BATTERED IN A FREAKISH CON-CENTRATION OF THE INTENSE RADIATION BANDS SURROUNDING HIS PLANET..."
"...HOW A TERRIBLE BLAST OF YELLOW LIGHT... SIMILAR TO THE AURORA BOREALIS -- BLINDED ME AT THE CONTROLS OF THE SHIP..."
"...AND CAUSED ME TO CRASH HELPLESSLY TO THE SUR-FACE OF HIS WORLD..."

"GATHERING MY FORCES, FIGHTING TO BREATHE, I MANAGED TO IMPART TO HIM CERTAIN NECESSARY INFORMATION..."
ONLY MOMENTS LEFT TO TELL YOU...ONCE YOU HAVE THE BATTERY YOU WILL HAVE POWER OVER EVERYTHING -- EXCEPT WHAT IS YELLOW!
THE UNIQUE METAL WHICH CHARGES THE BATTERY WITH ITS WONDROUS POWER HAS A YELLOW IMPURITY IN IT! STRANGELY ENOUGH, IF THE IMPURITY IS REMOVED, THE BATTERY LOSES ITS POWER!
IT IS THIS IMPURITY IN THE BATTERY WHICH MAKES IT POWERLESS AGAINST ANYTHING YELLOW!
I--I UNDERSTAND!
NOW TAKE MY RING...LET ME PUT IT ON YOU--! WITH THIS RING YOU WILL DRAIN POWER FROM THE BATTERY...
EFFECTIVE FOR 24 HOURS.. THEN YOU MUST RECHARGE IT AT THE BATTERY... VOWING EACH TIME TO USE IT AGAINST THE FORCES OF EVIL...!
NOW... I'VE TOLD YOU ALL... DO NOT FAIL... MY TRUST... UHH...UHH...
UHHHH...
GONE! HE... BREATHED HIS LAST!
AS THE CARTRIDGE CLICKS TO A STOP...
INCREDIBLE!...THAT'S THE WAY I BECAME A GREEN LANTERN! AT THE TIME, I THOUGHT I HAD GIVEN MYSELF THAT NAME -- BUT ACTUALLY IT WAS PLANTED IN MY MIND BY ABIN SUR!
AFTER HIS DEATH, I DONNED THE SPECIAL UNIFORM HE LEFT ME...
"...AND IN EXUBERANCE I TRIED OUT MY POWER RING FOR THE FIRST TIME..."
LIFTING A CLIFF INTO THE AIR! I CAN DO ANYTHING I WANT WITH THIS RING... ANYTHING I WILL TO HAPPEN... I CAN MAKE HAPPEN!
6

BUT WHAT ASTONISHES ME -- THERE WAS A CHANCE THAT ANOTHER EARTHMAN COULD HAVE BEEN CHOSEN TO BE A GREEN LANTERN!
I CAN'T HELP WONDERING WHAT WOULD HAVE HAPPENED IF THIS OTHER MAN-- THE SCHOOLTEACHER GUY GARDNER--HAD BEEN SELECTED BY ABIN SUR?
WE CAN SHOW YOU WHAT WOULD HAVE HAPPENED!
Y-YOU CAN--!?
INDEED! THIS MACHINE CAN COMPOSE DIFFERENT POSSIBILITIES IN THE FUTURE-- BASED ON ALTERNATE POSTULATES OF EVENTS!
LET US DEMONSTRATE, KA-- BY SCREENING THE ANSWER TO HIS QUESTION
THE PROPER INFORMATION HAS NOW BEEN PROGRAMMED INTO THE COMPUTER-CORE! WE WILL START IT AT THE HYPOTHETICAL MOMENT THAT GUY GARDNER-- INSTEAD OF YOURSELF-- WOULD HAVE BEEN CONTACTED BY THE STRICKEN ABIN SUR! THE MACHINE WILL ACT AS NARRATOR...
"PLUCKED FROM HIS POST AT SCHOOL... THE PHYSICAL EDUCATION INSTRUCTOR GUY GARDNER WAS WHISKED ACROSS THE COUNTRY..."
I'M IN THE GRIP OF SOMETHING THAT'S NOT OF THIS WORLD!
eh? THAT LOOKS LIKE AN ALIEN SPACECRAFT-- WRECKED!
IN HERE, GUY GARDNER..!
"SOON..."
YOU ARE HONEST... AND BORN WITHOUT FEAR!
USE THIS RING...AS GREEN LANTERN... AGAINST EVIL AND INJUSTICE!
I PROMISE--
I WILL DO MY BEST...
7

"AFTER THE DEATH OF ABIN SUR, THE NEW GREEN LANTERN TOOK OVER HIS UNIFORM AND TRIED HIS WINGS, FALTERINGLY AT FIRST..."
OOOF
I CAN'T GET THE HANG OF THIS RING! IT'S SO POWERFUL-- YET IT CAN SUDDENLY LOSE FORCE--!
I SEE WHAT WAS WRONG! I MUST WILL THE RING TO ACT PROPERLY!
I'VE GOT TO KEEP BACKING IT WITH MY WILL POWER WITHOUT A LETDOWN--!
WHAT A FEELING! TERRIFIC -- FANTASTIC!
"GUY RESUMED HIS NORMAL LIFE, CONCEALING THE THOUGHTS THAT NOW RACED THROUGH HIS MIND..."
NO ONE SHALL KNOW THAT I NOW HAVE A SECRET IDENTITY--AND THAT THE MOST IMPORTANT PART OF MY LIFE TAKES PLACE WHEN I DON MY GREEN LANTERN UNIFORM!
BY THE NUMBERS-- ONE--TWO--
"HIS FIRST CASE CAME DURING A RASH OF SABOTAGE IN EAST CITY..."
GREEN LANTERN IS GOING TO TAKE A CRACK AT THESE SABOTEURS!
NEWS
SABOTEURS STRIKE AGAIN! ARMS FACTORY BOMBED!
"THAT NIGHT AS THE EMERALD CRUSADER SCOURED THE CITY..."
MY RING'S DETECTED A HIDDEN RADIO TRANSMITTER IN THIS LOCALITY--COMING FROM THAT HOUSE...!
"INSTANTS LATER, A GREEN-CLAD PROJECTILE SPEARED THROUGH SOLID WALLS..."
TWO MORE FACTORIES DESTROYED, COMMANDER-- UH?
MY FIRST JOB-- I BETTER NOT MUFF IT!
CRASH!
8

"THE ENEMY AGENTS HAD NEVER CONFRONTED ANYONE LIKE GREEN LANTERN BEFORE! THEY THOUGH
BULLETS COULD STOP HIM..."
KILL HIM! HE MUST NOT LEAVE HERE ALIVE!
THIS GUY'S ANOTHER SUPERMAN! HE WHIPPED OUT A SHIELD--THAT'S STOPPING OUR BULLETS SHORT!
SPUNG!
"THEN GARDNER HURLED HIMSELF FORWARD..."
I DON'T TRUST MYSELF YET TO USE MY RING DIRECTLY ON THESE SABOTEURS--I MIGHT CRUSH THEM TO A PULP!
AND I WANT TO TURN THE OVER TO THE AUTHORITIES FOR QUESTIONING...ALIVE!
I'M IN TIP-TOP CONDITION--AS A PHYSICAL EDUCATION TEACHER SHOULD BE!
BUT I CAN'T SAY THE SAME FOR MY FOES--!
THEY'RE FLABBY-- WITH POOR REFLEXES!
KLOP!
FIGHT'S OVER!
I'LL SCOOP 'EM UP IN A POWER-RING NET AND HAND 'EM OVER TO THE F.B.I.!
9

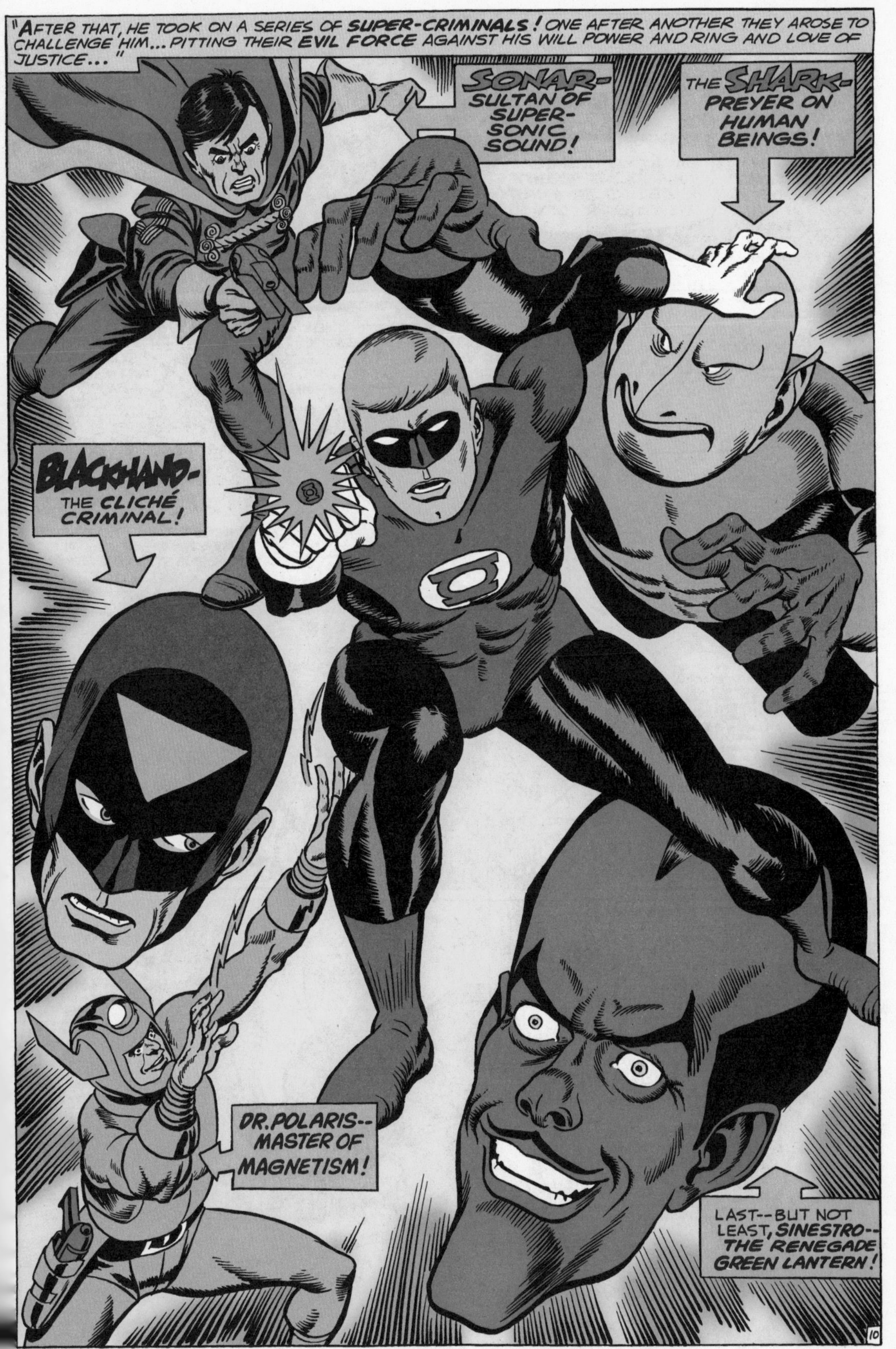
"AFTER THAT, HE TOOK ON A SERIES OF SUPER-CRIMINALS! ONE AFTER ANOTHER THEY AROSE TO CHALLENGE HIM... PITTING THEIR EVIL FORCE AGAINST HIS WILL POWER AND RING AND LOVE OF JUSTICE..."
SONAR-SULTAN OF SUPER-SONIC SOUND!
THE SHARK-PREYER ON HUMAN BEINGS!
BLACKHAND-THE CLICHÉ CRIMINAL!
DR. POLARIS--MASTER OF MAGNETISM!
LAST--BUT NOT LEAST, SINESTRO--THE RENEGADE GREEN LANTERN!
10

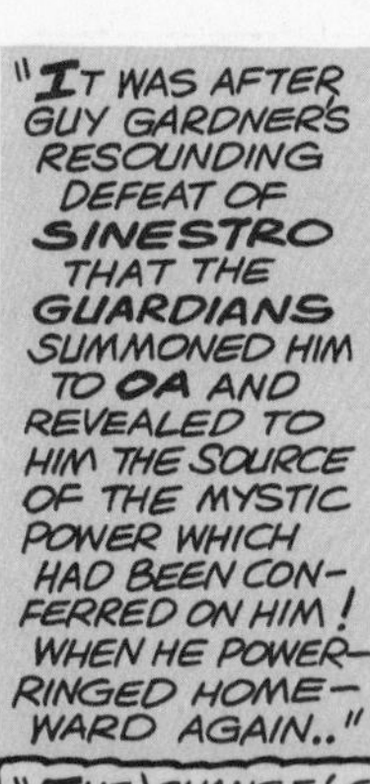
"IT WAS AFTER GUY GARDNER'S RESOUNDING DEFEAT OF SINESTRO THAT THE GUARDIANS SUMMONED HIM TO OA AND REVEALED TO HIM THE SOURCE OF THE MYSTIC POWER WHICH HAD BEEN CONFERRED ON HIM! WHEN HE POWER-RINGED HOMEWARD AGAIN.."

AN ASTONISHING ACCOUNT! SO FAR HIS CAREER VERY CLOSELY PARALLELS MY OWN--OR WOULD HAVE!
WAIT--I NOTICE HE'S TAKING A DIFFERENT ROUTE BACK TO EARTH--ONE I NEVER TOOK...
PERHAPS THIS "CHANGE" WILL BE SIGNIFICANT! LET US SEE...

"THE 'CHANGE' CAME WITH EXPLOSIVE SUDDENNESS!..."

BURSTS OF HIGH-POWERED ENERGY... EXPLODING ALL AROUND ME!

THEY'RE COMING FROM THAT ISOLATED PLANET AHEAD OF ME!

BY THE GALAXIES! A FANTASTIC DUEL BETWEEN ANTAGONISTS ARMED WITH RADIATION-WEAPONS!

IT WAS THOSE STRAY BLASTS FROM THE BATTLE THAT ALMOST STRUCK ME!

I WONDER IF I SHOULD MIX IN...?

IT MIGHT BE WORTH A GREEN LANTERN INVESTIGATION!

THAT ANSWERS MY QUESTION! THEY'RE TURNING THEIR WEAPONS ON ME!
INTRUDER--!
DESTROY HIM--!
11

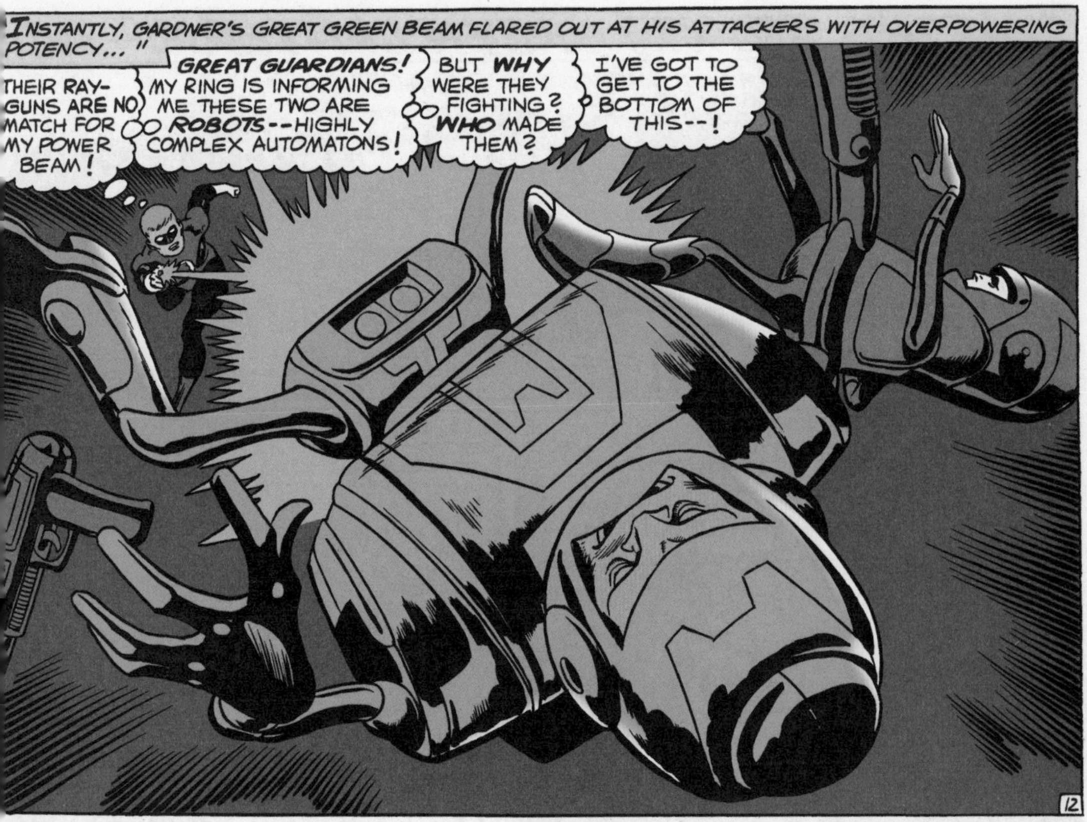

"INSTANTLY, GARDNER'S GREAT GREEN BEAM FLARED OUT AT HIS ATTACKERS WITH OVERPOWERING POTENCY... "

THEIR RAY-GUNS ARE NO MATCH FOR MY POWER BEAM!

GREAT GUARDIANS! MY RING IS INFORMING ME THESE TWO ARE ROBOTS--HIGHLY COMPLEX AUTOMATONS!

BUT WHY WERE THEY FIGHTING? WHO MADE THEM?

I'VE GOT TO GET TO THE BOTTOM OF THIS--!

12

"EARTH'S OTHER GREEN LANTERN!"--PART II

"HAVING SWIFTLY DISARMED HIS MECHANICAL FOES, THE RING-WIELDER PROBED THEIR COMPUTER-BRAINS..."

THIS PLANET, GHERA, IS INHABITED ONLY BY CHILDREN! THEY ARE THE ONLY HUMANS HERE...

CHILDREN--!?

YES... CHILDREN... WHO NEVER GROW OLD!

EONS AGO, THEIR GHERAN PARENTS WHO MADE US WERE WIPED OUT BY A TERRIBLE YELLOW PLAGUE!

SOMEHOW, ONLY THE CHILDREN REMAINED IMMUNE TO THE DISEASE! BUT IT HAD A STRANGE EFFECT ON THEM...

IT ARRESTED THEIR GROWTH! THEY NEVER GREW OLDER!

THAT'S AGAINST ALL THE LAWS OF NATURE--!

HUNGRY FOR RECREATION, THE AGELESS CHILDREN BEGAN PLAYING WAR GAMES! THEY DIVIDED INTO TWO ARMED CAMPS...

...ONE SIDE... MINE... CHOOSING ORANGE FOR ITS DISTINCTIVE COLOR...

...WHILE MY SIDE CHOSE BLUE!

EACH SIDE IS CONTINUALLY TRYING TO ANNIHILATE THE OTHER!

AS A RESULT, THIS WORLD IS ALWAYS AT WAR!

"LEAVING THE ROBOT PAIR IMMOBILIZED BY HIS BEAM, THE RING-WIELDER FLEW ONWARD ACROSS THE PLANET OF YOUTH..."

I MUST TRY TO END THE WAR HERE AND BRING PEACE!

WITHOUT PARENTS TO GUIDE THEM, THE CHILDREN HERE HAVE RUN WILD! THEY DON'T REALIZE THAT WAR AND DESTRUCTION ARE EVIL!

13

I'M SURE I CAN GET THE CHILDREN TO LISTEN TO REASON! I'LL BRING BOTH SIDES TOGETHER AND MAKE PEACE --eh?
A POWERFUL THOUGHT-WAVE REACHING ME!
SOME FORCE.. SEEKING TO CONTROL MY MIND!
GOT TO RESIST WITH ALL MY WILL POWER..!
THIS ONE HAS STRONG WILL POWER!
"DESPITE ALL HIS EFFORTS, GARDNER SUCCUMBED TO THE UNCANNY MENTAL ATTACK..."
WE'VE CAPTURED IT!
HOW EXCITING!
CAREFUL, GOR! BRING IT DOWN, CAREFULLY! DON'T DAMAGE IT!
"AND SHORTLY AFTERWARD..."
THE KIDS CLAMORING ALL AROUND ME..! THEY THINK I'M SOME NEW ROBOT-TOY!
AND I CAN'T MOVE... CAN'T LIFT A FINGER...!
IT IS BETTER THAN ANYTHING WE HAVE-- IT'S JUST LIKE A LIVING THING!
SOME SUPER-RACE MUST HAVE MADE IT!
CONTACT WITH THE BRAIN-CENTER INFORMS ME IT IS CALLED-- GREEN LANTERN!
14

"UNDER ABSOLUTE CONTROL OF THE BLUE COHORTS OF GHERA, THE 'TOY' CRUSADER WAS GIVEN A GRIM MISSION..."
...AND YOU WILL SEEK OUT THE ORANGE ARMY AND HELP US DEFEAT IT WITH YOUR TERRIFIC POWER RING!
THEN ALL THE ORANGERS MUST BE TAKEN PRISONER! IS THAT CLEAR?
TOO CLEAR! THEY'VE DRAFTED ME INTO THEIR ARMY!
GO, GREEN LANTERN-- CARRY OUT YOUR ASSIGNMENT TO THE BEST OF YOUR ABILITY!
I HAVE NO CHOICE!
"THUS, GARDNER FOUND HIMSELF FORCED TO TAKE PART IN THE PLANET-WIDE, DEADLY SERIOUS WAR GAME OF THE CHILDREN! HE WAS STILL OVER THE CITY WHEN SUDDENLY..."
A BIRD-CRAFT OF THE ORANGE ENEMY! SHOOT IT DOWN, GREEN LANTERN!
HURRY--BEFORE IT CAN ATTACK US!
"THE MYSTIC BEAM SWEPT OUT, CREATED A MIGHTY MOUNTAIN BEFORE THE WINGED SHIP--AND..."
KA-BOOM!
whew THAT'S A RELIEF! MY RING INFORMS ME THERE'S NOTHING ALIVE IN THERE -- IT'S ALL ROBOT-CONTROLLED!
YEEE! YEEE!
15

THE WAR GAME TOOK PLACE EVERYWHERE ON GHERA, EVEN UNDER THE SEA, WHERE SHORTLY HIS DIMINUTIVE MASTERS DISPATCHED THEIR NEW 'TOY' TO SEEK AND DESTROY A FANTASTIC ADVERSARY..."
A SUBMARINE IN THE SHAPE OF A HUGE FISH--HURLING LIGHTNING BOLTS AT ME!
I'VE NOT ONLY GOT TO DEFEND MYSELF--I HAVE TO COME UP WITH AN EFFECTIVE COUNTER-ATTACK OF MY OWN!
"FOR A WHILE IT SEEMED AS IF THE SPELL-BOUND GLADIATOR WAS DOOMED TO FAIL AGAINST HIS MONSTROUS, OMINOUS ADVERSARY..."
THOSE BOLTS DRIVING ME BACK--HARDLY GIVING ME A CHANCE TO WHIP UP MY WILL POWER--!
THEN--SHEER CONCENTRATION UNLEASHED A BLAST OF EMERALD ENERGY SO OVERWHELMING THAT..."
I'VE SHATTERED ITS DEFENSES! IT'S OUT OF CONTROL! QUIVERING AND SHAKING UNDER THE IMPACT OF INTERNAL EXPLOSIONS!
NOW TO MAKE SURE IT STAYS OUT OF ACTION--!
16

"WITH THE AID OF HIS GREAT BEAM, THE GUY-GREEN LANTERN LIFTED THE ENORMOUS FISH-SHAP
CRAFT ENTIRELY OUT OF THE WATER..."
IF THERE'S ONE PLACE A SUBMARINE WILL BE OUT OF ACTION -- IT'S HIGH AND DRY HERE ON THIS HILLTOP!
WELL DONE, GREEN LANTERN! YOU'RE READY FOR THE NEXT MOVE -- A DIRECT ATTACK ON THE LAND FORCES OF THE ORANGERS!
PRESS ON AT ONCE! WE WANT TOTAL VICTORY!
THE BLUE-KIDS STILL HAVE CONTROL OVER ME! -GASP- ISN'T THERE ANY WAY I CAN SHAKE OFF THEIR DOMINATION OF MY MIND?

LIKE A REMOTE-CONTROLLED TOY, THE EMERALD-GARBED CRUSADER SWEPT DEEPER INTO THE FRAY..."
I'D BE IN A TERRIBLE MESS IF THOSE DRAGON-LIKE TANKS WERE YELLOW INSTEAD OF ORANGE!
... DESTROY THE WARRIOR SENT AGAINST US BY THE BLUERS!

"THE GREEN GLADIATOR'S BATTLE PLAN WAS SIMPLICITY ITSELF-- FIGHT FIRE WITH FIRE ..."

AI! OUR TANKS BEING DEVOURED BY THEIR OWN TONGUES OF FLAME!

18

"IN DESPERATION, THE ORANGE CHILDREN SOUGHT TO WREST CONTROL OF GREEN LANTERN FROM THEIR BLUE FOES..."
ORM--CONTACT THEIR WARRIOR'S CONTROL-CENTER! DOMINATE IT!
GREAT GUARDIANS! I'M CAUGHT NOW IN A MENTAL TUG-OF-WAR!
GASP! IF THIS KEEPS UP, IT'LL SHATTER MY MIND! THE TWO-WAY PRESSURE... MOUNTING EVERY INSTANT...
KEEP CONTROL, GOR!
WHOEVER WINS THIS BATTLE, I LOSE--UNLESS I CAN USE THIS CLASH OF SUPER-MENTALITIES TO FREE MYSELF!
HARDER, ORM!
HERE GOES--WITH EVERY ERG OF WILL POWER I CAN SUMMON UP TO ACTIVATE MY RING!
"THEN, KEYED UP BY THE RESOLVE TO SAVE HIS LIFE--AND BRING PEACE TO THIS PLANET OF WAR-MINDED CHILDREN..."
DID IT!
DEFLECTED BOTH MENTAL BEAMS--FORCED THEM TO CLASH INTO EACH OTHER--LEAVING ME MOMENTARILY FREE OF EITHER ONE'S INFLUENCE!
"IN THA MOMENT OF FREEDOM, HE COATED HIMSELF WITH POWER-RING ARMOR..."
THERE--THAT OUGHT TO WITHSTAND EVEN THE MOST POWERFUL MENTAL ENERGY!
FROM NOW ON THIS GREEN LANTERN KNIGHT IS UNDER NOBODY'S CONTROL!

FREE TO ACT ON HIS OWN, GARDNER LOST NO TIME IN PACIFYING THE PLANET! IN THIS TASK HIS LONG EXPERIENCE AS A PUBLIC SCHOOL INSTRUCTOR ON EARTH STOOD HIM IN GOOD STEAD..."

BEGINNING TODAY, CHILDREN OF GHERA, LET YOUR GAMES BE GAMES OF ENJOYABLE SPORT AND EXERCISE--NOT OF HATEFUL WAR!
GREEN LANTERN IS RIGHT, GOR! OUR WAR GAMES WERE SILLY AND--STUPID!
I'M GLAD IT'S OVER, ORM!
OUR "TOY" TURNED OUT TO BE A HUMAN--AND A WISE HUMAN AT THAT--LIKE A FATHER!

I'VE USED MY POWER BEAM TO MAKE ALL THE CHILDREN OF GHERA NORMAL AGAIN! THEY WILL GROW UP NOW AND BECOME ADULTS--AND IN TIME THEY'LL HAVE CHILDREN OF THEIR OWN!
AS GREEN LANTERN SAID, LET THIS SHAKING OF HANDS BE A SIGN OF FRIENDSHIP!

GREEN LANTERN, WE'VE DECIDED ON A NEW FLAG FOR GHERA--
--WITH BLUE AND ORANGE COLORS--
--TO SYMBOLIZE THAT WE'VE JOINED TOGETHER--
--AND WON'T FIGHT EACH OTHER ANY MORE!

THEN MY JOB HERE IS DONE...
GOODBY, GREEN LANTERN!
PLEASE COME BACK FOR A VISIT...

"SHORTLY THE GREEN-CLAD CRUSADER ZOOMED SKYWARD WHENCE HE HAD COME..."
I WILL COME BACK ONE OF THESE DAYS AND CHECK ON THE CHILDREN TO MAKE SURE THEY'RE ALL RIGHT--BUT RIGHT NOW I'VE GOT TO HURRY!
IT'S ALMOST TWENTY-FOUR HOURS SINCE I LAST CHARGED MY RING ON OA! GOT TO GET BACK TO EARTH BEFORE I'M STRANDED THERE...!
20

"HE MADE IT ALL RIGHT, AND WITH HIS LAST SHREDS OF GREEN ENERGY REACHED HIS POWER BATTERY..."
ON WORLDS AFAR OR SCENES AT HOME, WHEREVER THE CAUSE SHOULD MAKE ME ROAM, ALWAYS I VOW TO FIGHT THE GOOD FIGHT-- TO COMBAT EVIL WITH ALL GREEN LANTERN'S MIGHT!

"BUT HARDLY HAD HE UTTERED THE OATH-- WHEN A TERRIBLE CHANGE CAME OVER HIM AND HE BEGAN TO SHAKE UNCON-TROLLABLY..."
CAN'T BREATHE-- -GASP!- I'VE TURNED ALL YELLOW!

"SUDDENLY HE REALIZED WHAT HAD OCCURRED..."
ON GHERA... SOMEHOW... I CAUGHT THE YELLOW PLAGUE!...
MY RING CAN'T HELP ME... NOTHING CAN HELP ME..!
I HAVE ONLY A SHORT WHILE LEFT TO LIVE... AND I KNOW WHAT I MUST DO...

"AS HAD THE DYING ABIN SUR BEFORE HIM, GARDNER IN EXTREMITY FOUND THE STRENGTH TO SHOOT OUT HIS POWER BEAM..."
...SEARCH FOR A DESERVING ONE... BRING HIM TO ME!... FIND ONE WHO IS HONEST AND BORN WITHOUT FEAR... GO... HURRY...

"FAST AS LIGHT, THE BEAM SPED ACROSS COUNTRY... AND RETURNED WITH THE DESERVING ONE IT HAD SELECTED..."
MY RING INFORMS ME... THIS YOUNG TEST PILOT IS DESTINED... TO BE-COME MY SUCCESSOR... THE NEW GREEN LANTERN OF EARTH!
HAL JORDAN... LISTEN TO ME...

I AM ABOUT TO DIE... AFTERWARD YOU WILL TAKE MY RING AND UNIFORM! AS GREEN LANTERN, YOU WILL COMBAT EVIL...
GREEN LANTERN--?
21

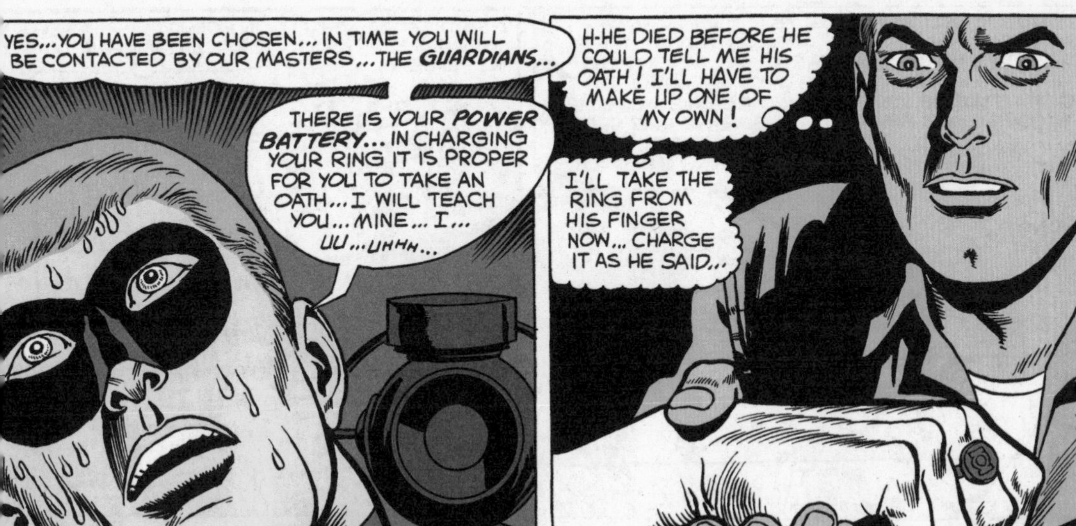
YES...YOU HAVE BEEN CHOSEN... IN TIME YOU WILL BE CONTACTED BY OUR MASTERS...THE GUARDIANS...
THERE IS YOUR POWER BATTERY... IN CHARGING YOUR RING IT IS PROPER FOR YOU TO TAKE AN OATH... I WILL TEACH YOU... MINE... I... UU...UHHH...
H-HE DIED BEFORE HE COULD TELL ME HIS OATH! I'LL HAVE TO MAKE UP ONE OF MY OWN!
I'LL TAKE THE RING FROM HIS FINGER NOW... CHARGE IT AS HE SAID...

"WITH WORDS THAT CAME TO HIM, HAL JORDAN CHARGED THE POWER RING.."
IN BRIGHTEST DAY, IN BLACKEST NIGHT, NO EVIL SHALL ESCAPE MY SIGHT! LET THOSE WHO WORSHIP EVIL'S MIGHT, BEWARE MY POWER-- GREEN LANTERN'S LIGHT!
"AND THUS AS A NEW GREEN LANTERN WAS BORN..."
THERE YOU HAVE IT, GREEN LANTERN OF EARTH! YOU HAVE SEEN WHAT WOULD HAVE HAPPENED IF THE OTHER DESERVING ONE ON YOUR PLANET HAD BEEN SELECTED BY ABIN SUR!
ASTONISHING...

IT SEEMS I WAS FATED TO BECOME GREEN LANTERN... ONE WAY OR ANOTHER!
I SHOULD LIKE TO MAKE THE ACQUAINTANCE OF GUY GARDNER-- IF IT IS PERMITTED...
PERMISSION GRANTED!

BACK ON EARTH... NOT LONG AFTERWARD...
THEN YOU TRAVEL A LOT, HAL?
THAT'S RIGHT, GUY! I USED TO BE A TEST PILOT BUT NOW I WORK FOR AN INSURANCE COMPANY!
I'LL ONLY BE HERE IN YOUR TOWN FOR A WEEK OR TWO...
ATHLETIC
22

IT WASN'T HARD TO MAKE GUY'S ACQUAINTANCE! I SIMPLY JOINED THIS ATHLETIC CLUB OF WHICH HE'S A MEMBER--AND IT DIDN'T TAKE US LONG TO BECOME GOOD FRIENDS!
KNOW SOME-THING, HAL? I'VE GOT THE STRANGEST FEELING WE'VE MET SOMEWHERE BEFORE--UNDER OTHER CIR-CUMSTANCES!
I JUST CAN'T SEEM TO REMEMBER...
HOW COULD HE--? IT NEVER REALLY HAPPENED!
I WISH I COULD TELL GUY HOW CLOSE HE CAME TO BECOMING GREEN LANTERN--
BUT I CAN'T!

SOON, A PARTING OF THE WAYS...
I'LL KEEP IN TOUCH WITH HIM!
IT ISN'T OFTEN IN LIFE THAT YOU COME ACROSS SOMEONE LIKE GUY GARDNER!
WE MAY NOT HAVE SEEN EACH OTHER BEFORE--BUT WE'LL SEE EACH OTHER AGAIN--I'LL MAKE SURE OF THAT!
THE END
23

GREEN LANTERN

# MUST THERE BE A SUPERMAN?

**Writer:** ELLIOT S. MAGGIN **Penciller:** CURT SWAN **Inker:** MURPHY ANDERSON

Originally presented in SUPERMAN No. 247, January 1972

Technically, you could argue on whether or not this is a GREEN LANTERN story. It was written by Elliot S. Maggin and illustrated by the great team of Curt Swan and Murphy Anderson for SUPERMAN #247. I debated for awhile about including this, but in the end felt it not only deserved to be reprinted somewhere, but it did showcase an aspect of the Guardians of the Universe that is amplified by being in a book like SUPERMAN.

At the very least, the title alone will pique your interest – "Must There Be a Superman?"

This is one of the most compelling and original stories about the existence of Superman on Earth and how his presence could be interpreted. In a lot of ways, Lex Luthor takes the Guardians' thoughts in this to an extreme. Is Superman holding back the progress of man? Is the world counting on him too much to solve their problems? Can we survive without Superman? Lex would go on to claim Superman was holding him back, but the Guardians have no such thoughts. As they state, they want to see life progress on planets naturally. Is Superman preventing that?

With this, Elliot redefined Superman's very reason for being on Earth, or maybe he shined a spotlight on it. Beyond the natural disasters and malicious beings, Superman is here to inspire more than anything else. We need to help ourselves and count on ourselves. Aliens, whether Superman or the Green Lantern Corps, can't solve the root of many of our problems. That's up to us.

Beyond being a strong story in its own right, this illustrates how far-reaching and powerful the Guardians of the Universe are. The Guardians are enigmatic in many ways, and that's part of their appeal. You're never quite sure where they're coming from, and often it appears they're making bizarre decisions. Combine that with Hal Jordan's lack of authority and you can have a lot of fun. But the fact that they appear in an issue of SUPERMAN in this role and judge him shows how far up the food chain they are.

They're a higher authority than even Superman.

– Geoff Johns

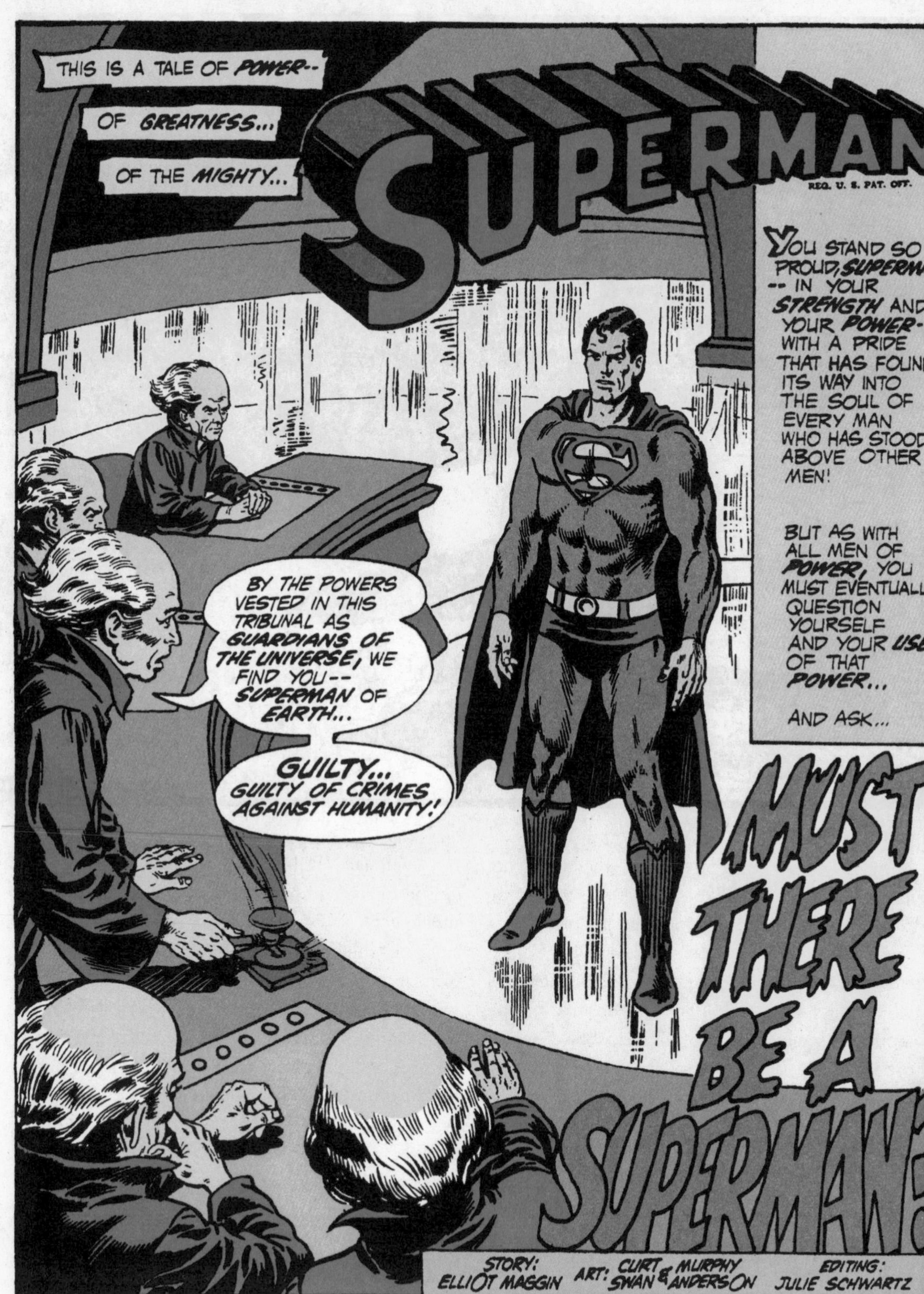

THIS IS A TALE OF POWER--
OF GREATNESS...
OF THE MIGHTY...
SUPERMAN
REG. U. S. PAT. OFF.
YOU STAND SO PROUD, SUPERM -- IN YOUR STRENGTH AND YOUR POWER- WITH A PRIDE THAT HAS FOUN ITS WAY INTO THE SOUL OF EVERY MAN WHO HAS STOOD ABOVE OTHER MEN!
BUT AS WITH ALL MEN OF POWER, YOU MUST EVENTUALL QUESTION YOURSELF AND YOUR US OF THAT POWER...
AND ASK...
BY THE POWERS VESTED IN THIS TRIBUNAL AS GUARDIANS OF THE UNIVERSE, WE FIND YOU-- SUPERMAN OF EARTH...
GUILTY... GUILTY OF CRIMES AGAINST HUMANITY!
MUST THERE BE A SUPERMAN?
STORY: ELLIOT MAGGIN ART: CURT SWAN & MURPHY ANDERSON EDITING: JULIE SCHWARTZ

THERE IT IS--JUST AS THE GUARDIANS SAID! A POD FULL OF SPORES BURSTING INTO OUR GALAXY!
IT WILL UPSET THE GALACTIC BALANCE OF NATURE IF IT IS ALLOWED TO GROW IN OUR UNIVERSE! I MUST BLAST IT OUT OF HERE!
IT'S GOING TO BE ROUGH! THIS PART OF THE GALAXY IS FULL OF RED STARS... LIKE THE STAR-SUN OF MY NATIVE KRYPTON!
I CAN ALREADY FEEL MY POWERS WEAKENING UNDER THEIR INFLUENCE!
BUT I CAN STILL WHIP UP ENOUGH SPEED AND FORCE TO DEFLECT THE POD...
UHH!
DIDN'T EVEN BUDGE IT!?
2

HAVE TO COME UP WITH ANOTHER WAY TO GET RID OF THAT BLASTED POD!... MY STRENGTH'S GOING FAST!

THAT RUNAWAY RED STAR MOVING OUT OF THE GALAXY--THAT'S IT!
IF THAT SPORE POD BEHAVES THE WAY I THINK IT DOES

...IT WILL BURST AND BEGIN TO SEED UPON CONTACT WITH A PLANET-LIKE ENVIRONMENT... AN ATMOSPHERE RICH IN GASES AND SUNLIGHT!
HAVE TO WORK FAST!

SO WHERE SHEER STRENGTH FAILED TO WORK, HOPEFULLY SUPER-WITS WILL SUCCEED, AS THE MAN OF STEEL FUSES MYRIADS OF METEOROIDS INTO A SMALL, DENSE PLANET...

...AND PROPELS THE MANMADE WORLD THROUGH A CROWDED SOLAR SYSTEM, WHERE IT CAPTURES AN ATMOSPHERE OF NITROGEN AND RARE GASES...

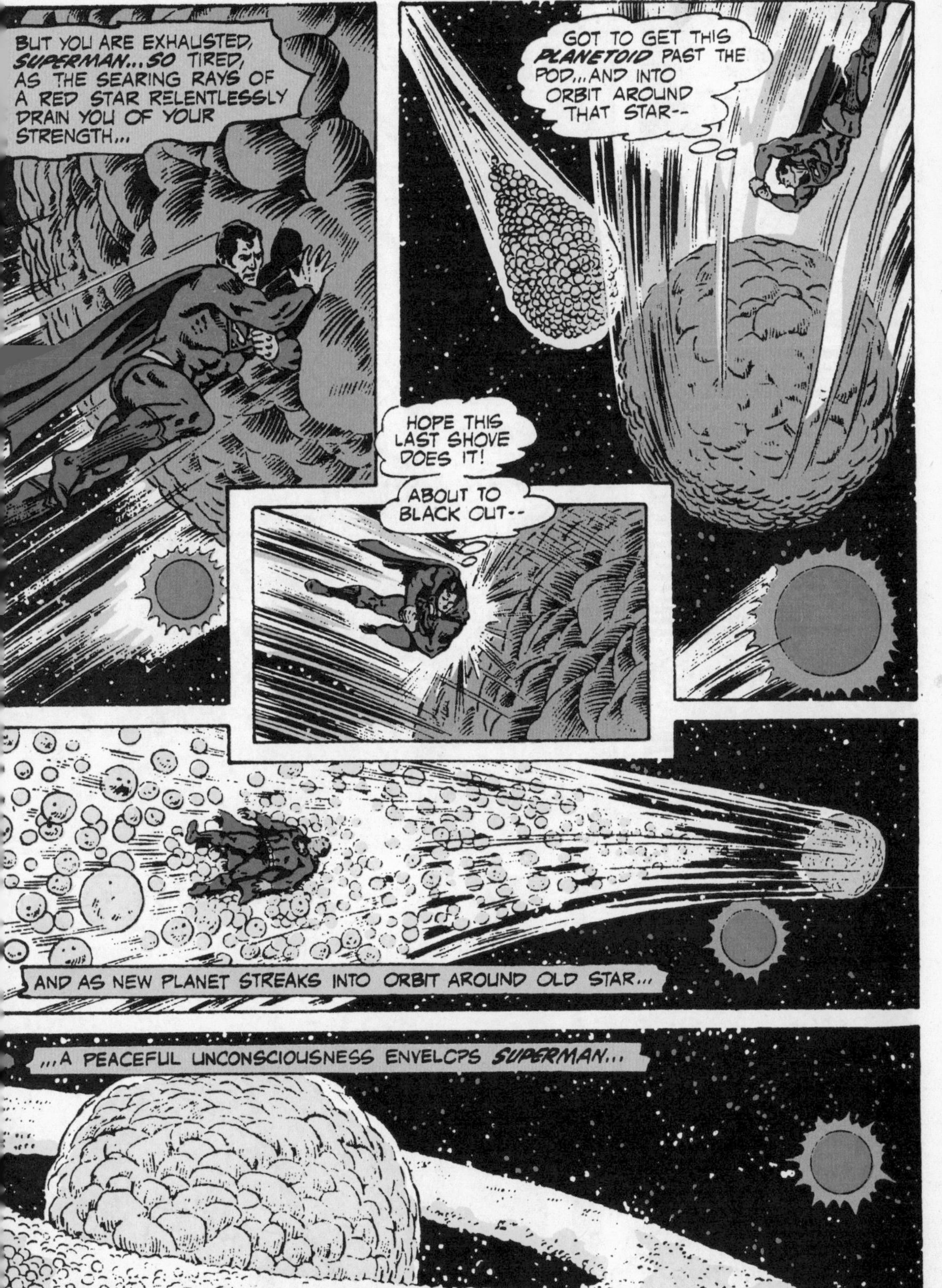
BUT YOU ARE EXHAUSTED, SUPERMAN...SO TIRED, AS THE SEARING RAYS OF A RED STAR RELENTLESSLY DRAIN YOU OF YOUR STRENGTH...
GOT TO GET THIS PLANETOID PAST THE POD,..AND INTO ORBIT AROUND THAT STAR--
HOPE THIS LAST SHOVE DOES IT!
ABOUT TO BLACK OUT--
AND AS NEW PLANET STREAKS INTO ORBIT AROUND OLD STAR...
...A PEACEFUL UNCONSCIOUSNESS ENVELOPS SUPERMAN...
4

BOW YOUR HEADS AND CATCH YOUR BREATH, HUMANS--

FOR YOU ARE ABOUT TO COME INTO THE AWESOME PRESENCE OF...

...THE GUARDIANS OF THE UNIVERSE!
EXCELLENT RESCUE, KATMA TUI-- GREEN LANTERN OF KORUGAR!
PLACE THE KRYPTONIAN ON THE SOLIDIFIED LIGHT-BEAMS AND THEN-- DEPART!
I HOPE HE RECOVERS!
HE WILL!

THE GUARDIANS--A RACE OF IMMORTALS--WHOSE SELF-APPOINTED TASK IS TO SURVEY AND SAFEGUARD THE 100 BILLION STARS OF THE MILKY WAY GALAXY AND THE LIVES THAT GROW IN THEIR LIGHT...
FOR THE ARCHIVES! KAL-EL, THE SUPERMAN OF EARTH...

...IS NOW UNDERGOING THE HEALING PROCESS FOR INJURIES SUSTAINE WHILE UNDERTAKING OUR SPECIAL MISSION...
THESE ARE THE SELF-SAME GUARDIANS WHO HAVE DISPATCHED THE GREEN LANTERN CORPS TO SERVE AS THEIR DEPUTIES ACROSS THE BREADTH OF THE GALAXY...

UPON DETERMINING THE YELLOW NATURE OF THE POD-MENACE-- AGAINST WHICH THE LANTERNS' POWER RINGS WOULD BE INEFFECTUAL-- WE JUDGED THAT..

...THIS WAS A JOB FOR SUPERMAN!

NOW THAT KAL-EL IS IN OUR MIDST, WE HAVE DECIDED TO IMPLANT IN HIS SUBCONSCIOUS THE NOTION THAT HIS INFLUENCE ON EARTH IS INTERFERING WITH HUMAN PROGRESS:

LET THE OPERATION BEGIN...!

WH-WHERE AM I? THE SPORES! DID I--?
YOU ARE IN THE CORE OF OUR MAIN POWER BATTERY-- THE ENERGY-SOURCE OF THE GREEN LANTERNS' POWER RINGS!
YOU SUCCESSFULLY ELIMINATED THE SPORE-POD DANGER.. BUT SUFFERED INJURY TO YOURSELF..

IT IS ESSENTIAL YOU STAY HERE ON OA TO RECUPERATE!
PERHAPS YOU WOULD LIKE TO SEE OUR CENTER OF OPERATIONS?
YES, I'D LIKE THAT! GREEN LANTERN TOLD ME A BIT OF YOUR SET-UP HERE...

PLEASE UNDERSTAND, KAL-EL, WE HAVE ALWAYS RESPECTED YOU-- NONETHELESS, YOUR INTERFERENCE WITH HUMAN SOCIAL GROWTH--
MY-- WHAT? WHAT ARE YOU TALKING ABOUT?
6

SURELY YOU MUST REALIZE THAT YOUR PRESENCE ON EARTH DIRECTLY CONTRIBUTES TO THE TERRANS' CULTURAL LAG!
CULTURAL LAG?--I STILL DON'T UNDER-STAND!

PERHAPS WE SHOULD NOT CONFRONT THE KRYPTONIAN WITH SUCH CONCEPTS!
REMEMBER THAT, UNLIKE HIM, THE GUARDIANS' INFLUENCE ON PLANETARY CULTURE IS INDIRECT--!
AGREED! I SHALL DISCONTINUE THE SUBJECT!
I HOPE KAL-EL HASN'T OVERHEARD

WE WILL NOW PROCEED TO THE HALL OF RECORDS--IF THAT IS TO YOUR LIKING--?
HUH?--OKAY... SURE...
EXCELLENT! HIS REACTION REVEALS HE DID OVER-HEAR US!

DIRECT CAUSE... CULTURAL LAG...?
IN THIS SPHERE IS STORED THE COMPLETE HISTOR OF THE GALAXY...

INDIRECT INFLUENCE ON PLANETARY CULTURES...?
WHA...? OH--UH-HUH...
WOULD YOU LIKE A DEMONSTRATION...?

PERHAPS SOME RECENT HISTORY--SUCH AS THE TIME YOU VISITED THE PLANET KALYARNA WITH THE JUSTICE LEAGUE OF AMERICA?*
FINE--

*NOTE: THAT WAS IN JUSTICE LEAGUE #8

SEE AGAIN... HEAR AGAIN-- YOUR WARNING TO THE KALYARNANS...
NOW THAT YOU'RE HERE, SUPERMAN, YOU CAN SAVE OUR PLANET!

YOU'VE MISSED THE POINT! YOU'LL NEVER SOLVE THE PROBLEM BY HANDING IT TO SOMEBODY ELSE!

MY COLLEAGUES AND I WILL RESTORE YOUR SEAS' ECOLOGY... BUT WHATEVER WE DO CAN ONLY BE TEMPORARY...

YOU MUST EACH FACE YOUR OWN PROBLEMS-- REDO YOUR THINKING ABOUT HOW AND WHY YOU POLLUTE YOUR PLANET...

"EVEN AS WE MUST DO ON EARTH!"
HMMM--
8

PRESENTLY...
IT HAS BEEN A PRODUCTIVE VISIT, KAL-EL!
FAREWELL--
GLAD TO HAVE BEEN OF SERVICE--
CAN'T GET IT OUT OF MY MIND! ME-- HOLDING BACK SOCIAL GROWTH?

OUR PLAN IS PROGRESSING HIS BEHAVIOR PATTERN INDICATES THAT OUR PLANTED IDEA IS BEGINNING TO GROW IN HIS MIND!
HE AND HIS ADOPTED PLANET WILL SOON BE THE BETTER FOR IT!

EVEN AS HE HURTLES EARTHWARD, SUPERMAN'S TROUBLESOME THOUGHTS CONTINUE TO GROW IN HIS BRAIN...
AM I AS MUCH A DISTURBING FORCE ON EARTH'S NATURAL PROGRESS AS THOSE SPORES WOULD HAVE BEEN ON THE ENTIRE GALAXY?

FOR YEARS I'VE BEEN PLAYING BIG BROTHER TO THE HUMAN RACE! HAVE I BEEN WRONG? ARE THEY DEPENDING ON ME TOO MUCH... TOO OFTEN...?

THUS, IT IS A CONFUSED SUPERMAN WHO POWER-DIVES TO EARTH OVER CENTRAL CALIFORNIA...
YEAH... MAYBE I HAVE BEEN INTERFERING UNNECESSARILY!
I DECIDE WHAT'S RIGHT OR WRONG--AND THEN ENFORCE MY DECISION... BY BRUTE STRENGTH!

FURTHER-MORE, I--
HUNH?
YOU WON'T PICK ANY PEACHES, HEY? THIS WILL MAKE YOU CHANGE YOUR MIND!
SLAAP!
P-PLEASE, SEÑOR HARLEY-- STOP IT!
OHH... WON'T SOMEONE HELP ME?

HOLD IT! KEEP YOUR HANDS OFF THAT KID!
LET 'IM HAVE IT, SUPERMAN! GIVE IT TO HIM GOOD!
S-SUPERMAN-- DON'T INTERFERE! YOU HAVE NO RIGHT--

THOUGH WE HAD ALL AGREED TO STRIKE, EVERYONE BUT ME WENT BACK TO WORK WHEN SEÑOR HARLEY WARNED HE'D FIRE US!
YOU SAW HARLEY BEATING UP MANUEL, SUPERMAN! MASH HIM!
10

YOU FELLOWS WERE HERE! WHY DIDN'T YOU HANDLE IT?

AND AS FOR YOU, MR. HARLEY-- THE LAW WILL--
LET GO OF ME-- OR I'LL HAVE YOU ARRESTED! I'M BOSS HERE--I KNOW MY LEGAL RIGHTS!

DON'T LISTEN TO THAT PIG, SUPER-MAN!
SHOW HARLEY WHO'S THE REAL BOSS, HERE!
THROW HIM IN JAIL!
CUT THAT KIND OF TALK!
YOU'RE ALL PRETTY BRAVE NOW THAT I'M HERE--!

LISTEN, MANUEL-- I WON'T FIND OUT WHAT'S BEEN GOING ON FROM THESE HOTHEADS! TELL ME YOUR STORY...YOUR PROBLEM--
SEÑOR SUPERMAN-- I COME FROM MEXICO! AS MY FATHER LAY DYING, HE TOLD ME TO COME TO THE U.S.A. FOR A BETTER LIFE...

WHO KNOWS WHAT SETS OFF A MEMORY BURIED DEEPLY IN THE MIND OF A SUPERMAN...?
...A MEMORY OF ANOTHER PLACE, LONG AGO AND FAR AWAY... AND ANOTHER FATHER-- HIS OWN...

...JOR-EL-- WHO JUST BEFORE HE DIED SAW TO IT THAT HIS SON MIGHT HAVE A CHANCE AT A BETTER LIFE...

FLASHING MEMORIES THAT ONLY MOMENTARILY INTERRUPT THE MAN OF STEEL-- FOR THERE IS WORK TO BE DONE...
...BUT HERE I AM, JUST A FIELD-PICKER... AND LIFE IS THE SAME AS BEFORE--
YET, MANUEL... YOU WERE THE ONLY ONE WITH THE COURAGE TO STRIKE!
WILL YOU SHOW ME WHERE YOU LIVE?

MAMMA! MAMMA! SUPER-HOMBRE!
HE IS HERE!
SHH! DO NOT TALK NONSENSE, JUAN--

CARAMBA!
12

WITHIN MOMENTS, A CROWD OF HERO-WORSHIPERS SWARMS AROUND THE VISITING CELEBRITY...
MY HOUSE-- JUST LOOK AT IT! THE ROOF IS FALLING IN! BUILD ME A NEW ONE!
GRACIAS A DIOS YOU HAVE COME HERE! NOW YOU CAN SOLVE ALL OUR PROBLEMS--!
SI! FIRST YOU PUT SEÑOR HARLEY IN JAIL--LIKE HE DESERVES!

...AND IF YOU REBUILT EVERY GHETTO AND ARRESTED EVERY SLUM-LORD? WHAT THEN, SUPERMAN?

WELL--WHEN YOU GOING TO START, SUPERMAN?
RIGHT NOW! AND WHAT I'M GOING TO DO IS--

NOTHING!
NOTHING AT ALL!

WHATEVER HELP YOU CLAIM YOU NEED--MUST COME FROM YOURSELVES--
--EH? THOSE BIRDS--IN WILD FLIGHT! IT MUST MEAN THAT--

EARTHQUAKE--!
THIS GROVE IS CLOSE TO THE SAN ANDREAS FAULT--CALIFORNIA'S EARTHQUAKE BELT!

NOT EVEN A SUPERMAN CAN STOP AN EARTHQUAKE, BUT HE MIGHT BLUNT IT--

WHEN UNDERGROUND ROCKS PUSH AGAINST EACH OTHER IN OPPOSITE DIRECTIONS AS THE EARTH MOVES, THEY KEEP STRETCHING--
--AND WHEN THEY CAN STRETCH NO MORE, THEY BREAK... AND THE EARTH QUAKES!
14

THE BREAKING POINT OF THE EARTHQUAKE-- A RIP IN THE MAKE-UP OF THE PLANET-- WHERE JAGGED ROCKS CRASHING AGAINST EACH OTHER SHAKE A PLANET--
IF I CAN EASE THE TENSION BELOW THE SURFACE BY SMOOTHING THE WALLS OF THIS FISSURE, THE QUAKE SHOULD SUBSIDE MORE EASILY...

MY ACTIVITY DOWN HERE IS CAUSING MORE ROCKS TO FLY AROUND... CAUSING MORE TENSION...
HAVE TO STOP THAT--

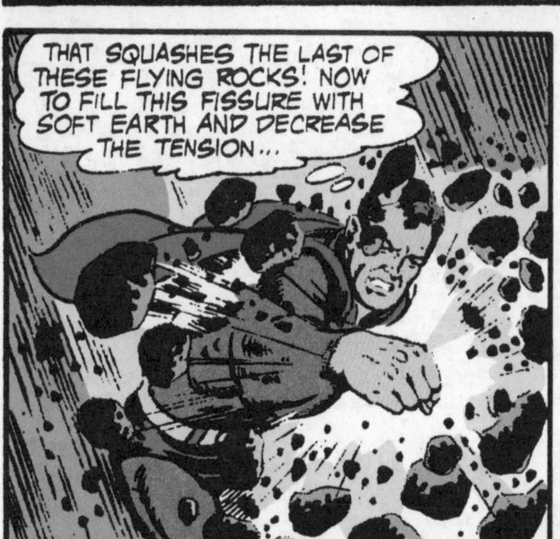
THAT SQUASHES THE LAST OF THESE FLYING ROCKS! NOW TO FILL THIS FISSURE WITH SOFT EARTH AND DECREASE THE TENSION...

THIS FLAT BOULDER MAKES A HANDY SHOVEL!

THEN, AS SUPERMAN BURSTS OUT OF THE EARTH'S CRUST...
SEÑOR SUPERMAN! OUR HOUSES-- THEY HAVE ALL FALLEN DOWN!
YOU WILL PUT THEM UP FOR US AGAIN, SI?
HOW CAN I TELL THEM NOW THAT THEY MUST BE SELF-SUFFICIENT--

--WHEN I HAVE TO REBUILD THEIR HOMES FOR THEM?
VIVA SUPERMAN!

OUR NEW HOMES!
GRACIAS--
COME BACK HERE--ALL OF YOU!
I WAS SAYING SOMETHING BEFORE THE NOISE STARTED--AND THIS TIME YOU'RE GOING TO LISTEN--
--COME HELL OR ANOTHER EARTHQUAKE!

SUPERMAN--YOU HAVE STOPPED AN EARTHQUAKE... REBUILT OUR HOMES! THERE IS MORE YOU WANT TO DO FOR US--?
LET'S GET SOMETHING STRAIGHT! SURE--I REBUILT YOUR HOMES, BUT THAT WAS BECAUSE AN EARTHQUAKE IS SOMETHING YOU CAN'T HANDLE--SOMETHING YOU CAN'T SAFEGUARD YOURSELVES AGAINST--

BUT YOU MUST NOT COUNT ON A SUPERMAN TO PATCH UP YOUR LIVES EVERY TIME YOU HAVE A CRISIS--OR DISASTER--
YOUNG MANUEL HERE--HAS THE RIGHT IDEA! WHEN THE REST OF YOU BACKED DOWN TO HARLEY, MANUEL REFUSED TO KNUCKLE UNDER...

YOU DON'T NEED A SUPERMAN!
WHAT YOU REALLY NEED IS A SUPER-WILL TO BE GUARDIANS OF YOUR OWN DESTINY!
NOW I'VE GOT WORK OF MY OWN TO DO...

SOB YOU LEAVING ALREADY, SUPERMAN?
YES, MANUEL--BUT WE'LL KEEP IN TOUCH!
16

YOU CAN REACH ME AT GALAXY BROADCASTING IN METROPOLIS-- WILL YOU DO THAT?
SI!-- YES...I PROMISE!

YOU SOUNDED GOOD BACK THERE, SUPERMAN- BUT DID YOU REALLY BELIEVE ALL THAT BIG TALK?...
WGBS

THEN--HOW COME YOUR MIND IS LIGHT-YEARS AWAY AS YOU INSTINCTIVELY RUSH TOWARD A NEW EMERGENCY...?
ARE YOU HAVING SECOND THOUGHTS ABOUT A PLANET YOU NEVER REALLY COULD IMAGINE TAKING CARE OF ITSELF WITHOUT YOU...?
BULLETIN: PLEASURE CRUISER ENDANGERED BY WATER SPOUT IN MID-ATLANTIC...

KAL-EL IS TROUBLED SOMEWHAT BY AN IDEA THAT NEVER CROSSED HIS MIND BEFORE-- THE FACT THAT PEOPLE OF EARTH MUST PROGRESS UNAIDED BY OUTSIDERS FROM OTHER WORLDS...
17
HERE COMES SUPERMAN! HE'LL SAVE US!
THEN OUR TASK IS DONE! WE MUST LET TIME TAKE ITS COURSE!

## APPRENTICE

**Writer:** TODD KLEIN **Artist:** DAVE GIBBONS

## PROGRESS

**Writer:** JOEY CAVALIERI **Artist:** DAVE GIBBONS

## FINAL DUTIES

**Writer:** LEN WEIN **Artist:** GIL KANE

## I, LANTERN

**Writer:** JOEY CAVALIERI **Artist:** KEVIN O'NEILL

Originally presented in GREEN LANTERN No. 162, 173, 177, 182 and 183, 1983-1984

## WHAT PRICE HONOR?

**Writer:** TODD KLEIN **Artist:** DAVE GIBBONS **Inker:** RAY MCCARTHY

Originally presented in GREEN LANTERN CORPS QUARTERLY No. 6, Fall 1993

the early '80s, TALES OF THE GREEN LANTERN CORPS was regular backup feature in GREEN LANTERN. These stories intro-uced and explored dozens of alien officers within the Corps. ney also reexamined what it meant to be chosen by the power ng. And what it took to become a true Green Lantern. Overcoming fear, aspiring for truth and honor and fighting to the eath if need be.

I wrote earlier about some of the writers and artists that may ot have been as well known for their incredible contributions to REEN LANTERN. In particular, I'd like to single out Todd Klein nd Joey Cavalieri.

I have never had the pleasure to meet Todd, but he is best own for being one of the greatest, if not the greatest, letterer d logo designer in the industry. He's like the Jack Kirby of let-ring. However, Todd also wrote quite a few stories for DC omics in the 80s, including a long run on Omega Men and a ew of back-ups for GREEN LANTERN. One of them, pprentice," is presented here. This is only one example of the tention Todd paid to these officers who had mostly been filling the background for decades. This is where the Green Lantern orps truly started to take shape.

Joey Cavalieri I've known for a long, long time. He was my itor, and currently is, on THE FLASH. But before I knew him, I ew his work. Specifically his brilliant work on GREEN NTERN. "Progress" is one of my favorite short stories in comics all time, and with "I, Lantern" Joey crafted a tale that wonder-y defined the robotic Lantern, Stel. Joey went on to write sever-more issues of GREEN LANTERN, and it is his work that most pired mine in GREEN LANTERN: REBIRTH. Joey was the first e to explore the yellow impurity within the Central Power ttery and had Sinestro make contact with it. This was the main plot point in REBIRTH, and the growth of Parallax and the emotional spectrum grew from there. In my mind, Joey Cavalieri is right up there with John Broome, Alan Moore and Dave Gibbons in what they've done for the mythology of the Green Lantern Corps.

A writer who needs no introduction, Len Wein is recognized for the creation of SWAMP THING and Wolverine, among many others. But he also wrote some of the most poignant and elegant tales of the Green Lantern, including the short story "Final Duties," illustrated by Gil Kane.

There were two other amazing artists, along with Gil Kane, who defined the world of GREEN LANTERN: Dave Gibbons and Kevin O'Neill. Dave's work on GREEN LANTERN would continue for decades, most recently reintroducing and restarting the GREEN LANTERN CORPS title as a writer and artist after REBIRTH. Dave was also my main collaborator on SINESTRO CORPS on the writing end. Kevin O'Neill created a truly alien world, one they could only dream of replicating on the big screen. Kevin would go on to illustrate a very important story that would redefine Abin Sur.

Finally, I've also included a longer "Tales of the Green Lantern Corps" story by Ruben Diaz and Travis Charest. It's breath-takingly beautiful. Travis Charest is an artist who did some work for DC in the '90s before exploding into one of the top talents in the medium. In "What Price Honor?" they introduced a Green Lantern who has become a very prominent character within the mythos, Laira. She has since gone on to join the Red Lanterns.

The most compelling Green Lanterns can come from anywhere.

– Geoff Johns

Very late it was, my little.
So late, that ALL the moons beamed down upon the youngling as he crept into the master's room.
You know how late THAT is.
But he wasn't sleepy, oh MY no!
LONG had he planned this as he worked for the master: cleaning and cooking, listening and learning.
The ring, the brightly shining RING OF POWER! So many lessons learned, but never a PIP of what he so desired!
He could wait no longer, this youngling.
The master would NEVER KNOW... there would be PLENTY of time for returning.
Or so he hoped, my little.
GREEN LANTERN CORPS
"apprentice"
TODD KLEIN, STORY & LETTERS * DAVE GIBBONS, ARTIST * NANSI HOOLAHAN, COLORS * COLÓN, EDITOR *

AT LAST, AT LAST!
SLEEP AWAY, OLD MASTER, WHILE MIGHTY DEETER WIELDS THE RING!

LET THE EVIL ONES COWER AND MEWL AS I GO AT THEM...

...THUS...?

HUMPH. THIS WILL NEVER DO.

Grinching down, he tries harder!
PIT
PIT
PIT
FIPP!
UG!
FLIPP!
PIT
THAT'S BETTER... BUT PERHAPS IT WILL TAKE SOME PRACTICE.

Practice he DOES, until the night is ABLAZE with his practicings! The oldsters point and mumble.
"Be strange doin's tonight," they noddle.
Well away they keep, to be sure.

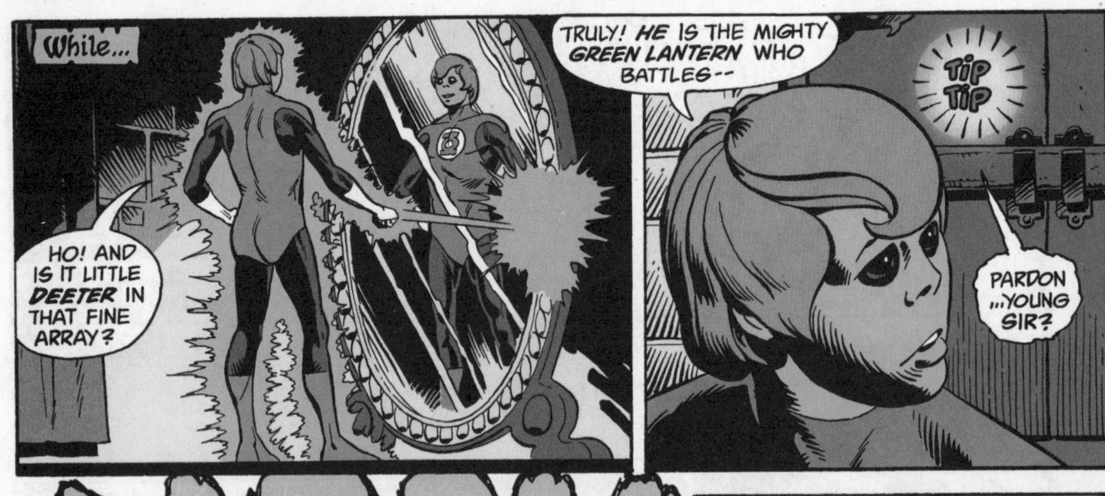
While...
HO! AND IS IT LITTLE DEETER IN THAT FINE ARRAY?
TRULY! HE IS THE MIGHTY GREEN LANTERN WHO BATTLES--
TIP TIP
PARDON ...YOUNG SIR?

WH-WH- WHU-WHU--!?

AH. JUST WHAT I NEED ON A COLD NIGHT--
--WARM BLOOD, AND A NICE GREEN FIRE!

OH, PLEASE, RING, HEED ME NOW...
As never before, he grinches...

--and ATTACKS! The bright beams SPLASH across the beast...

...and fell him NOT.

HEE! HEH! GOOD, YOUNGLING. I FEEL BETTER ALREADY.
NOW A FEW LANTERN BONES FOR SPICE!

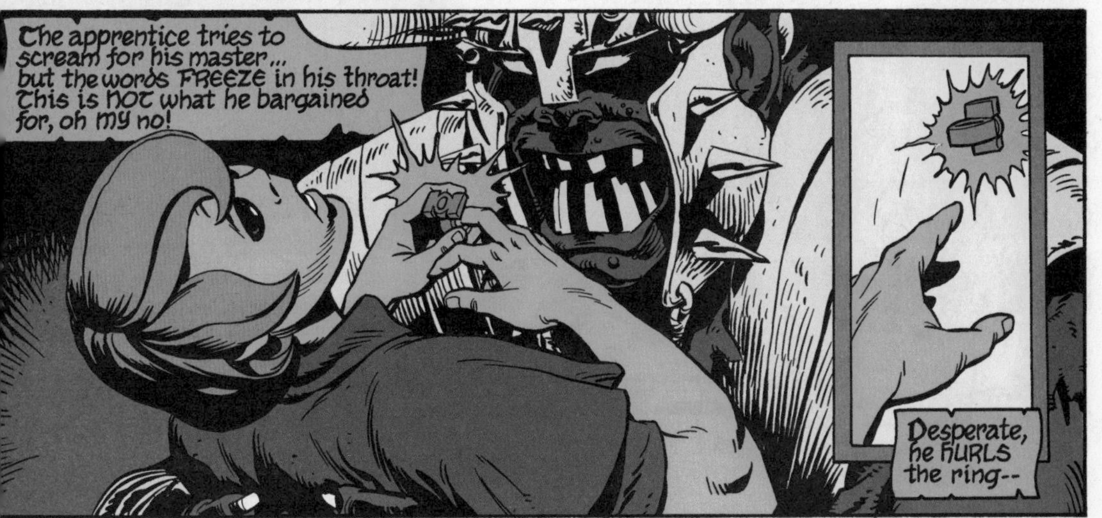
The apprentice tries to scream for his master... but the words FREEZE in his throat! This is NOT what he bargained for, oh my no!
Desperate, he HURLS the ring--

-- and ANOTHER hand is there to pick it up.

Just in time the master has come. Deeter wearies a sigh.

Never has he been so glad to see that stern, angry glare-- even though he knows what will come after!

TH-THERE I WAS, O WONDERFUL MASTER, JUST CLEANING YOUR RING FOR TOMORROW, WHEN--
--CRASH! THE BEAST CAME RIGHT THROUGH THE DOOR! NATURALLY, I WAS FURIOUS, KNOWING HOW MUCH YOU LIKED THE DOOR, BUT I DIDN'T WANT TO WAKE YOU, SO--

ENOUGH! I SEE A FOOLISH APPRENTICE. I SEE A MOLLUCKING GREAT CLUTTER.

GO, BRATLING, AND GET THY MOP, SO THAT ONE MAY TAKE CARE OF THE OTHER!

So he labored, while the TRUE Green Lantern smiled just a little at a lesson well taught. So he labored 'til ALL the suns arose again. You know how long THAT is.

Think of this, my little, should you ever scamper off again to the Green Lantern's house.

I remember well that he was no EASY one to work for. But then neither am I. Oh my no.

END.

# PROGRESS

JOEY CAVALIERI
WRITER
DAVE GIBBONS
ARTIST
JEANINE CASEY
COLORIST
LEN WEIN
EDITOR

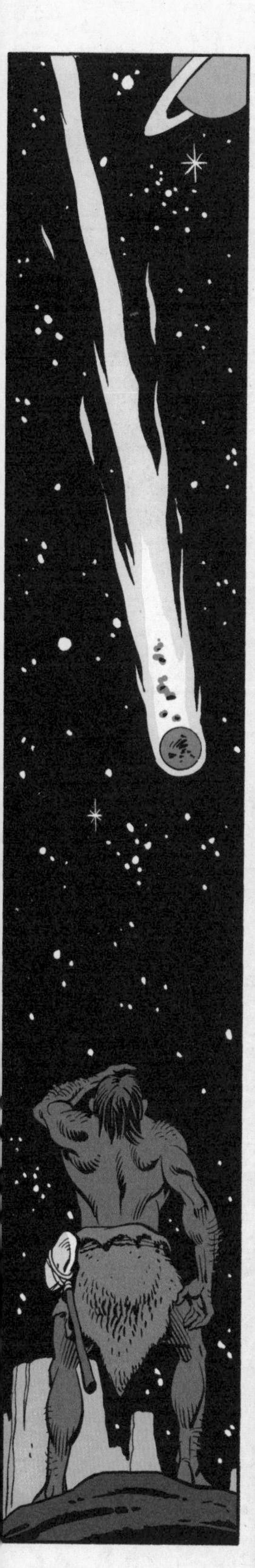

AND SO IT GOES...

TALES OF THE GREEN LANTERN CORPS
"FINAL DUTIES"
LEN WEIN WRITER/EDITOR * GIL KANE ARTIST * BEN ODA LETTERER * ANTHONY TOLLIN COLORIST
KWO VARRIKK'S FINAL DAY AS A MEMBER OF THE PROUD GREEN LANTERN CORPS BEGINS AS HAD ALL THE OTHERS--
--WITH THE RISING OF HIS HOMEWORLD'S BUOYANT CRIMSON SUN, THE CHARGING OF HIS POWER RING, AND THE RECITING OF HIS ANCIENT SACRED OATH...
THE RITUAL COMPLETED, HE PAUSES AT HIS WINDOW FOR A MOMENT, TAKING IN THE SUMMER-SWEET SCENT OF THE DISTANT D'BALLAH TREES AND THE CRYSTAL SONG OF THE FEATHERED WINDFLYTES IN THEIR BRANCHES...
EVEN FOR ONE WHO HAS TRAVERSED THE COSMOS, THERE COULD BE NO BETTER PLACE TO LIVE OUT THE REMAINDER OF ONE'S DAYS, HE SMILES--
--AND HE THINKS:
TIME ENOUGH FOR CONTEMPLATION LATER!
THERE IS MUCH TO BE ACCOMPLISHED BEFORE THIS PRECIOUS DAY IS DONE!

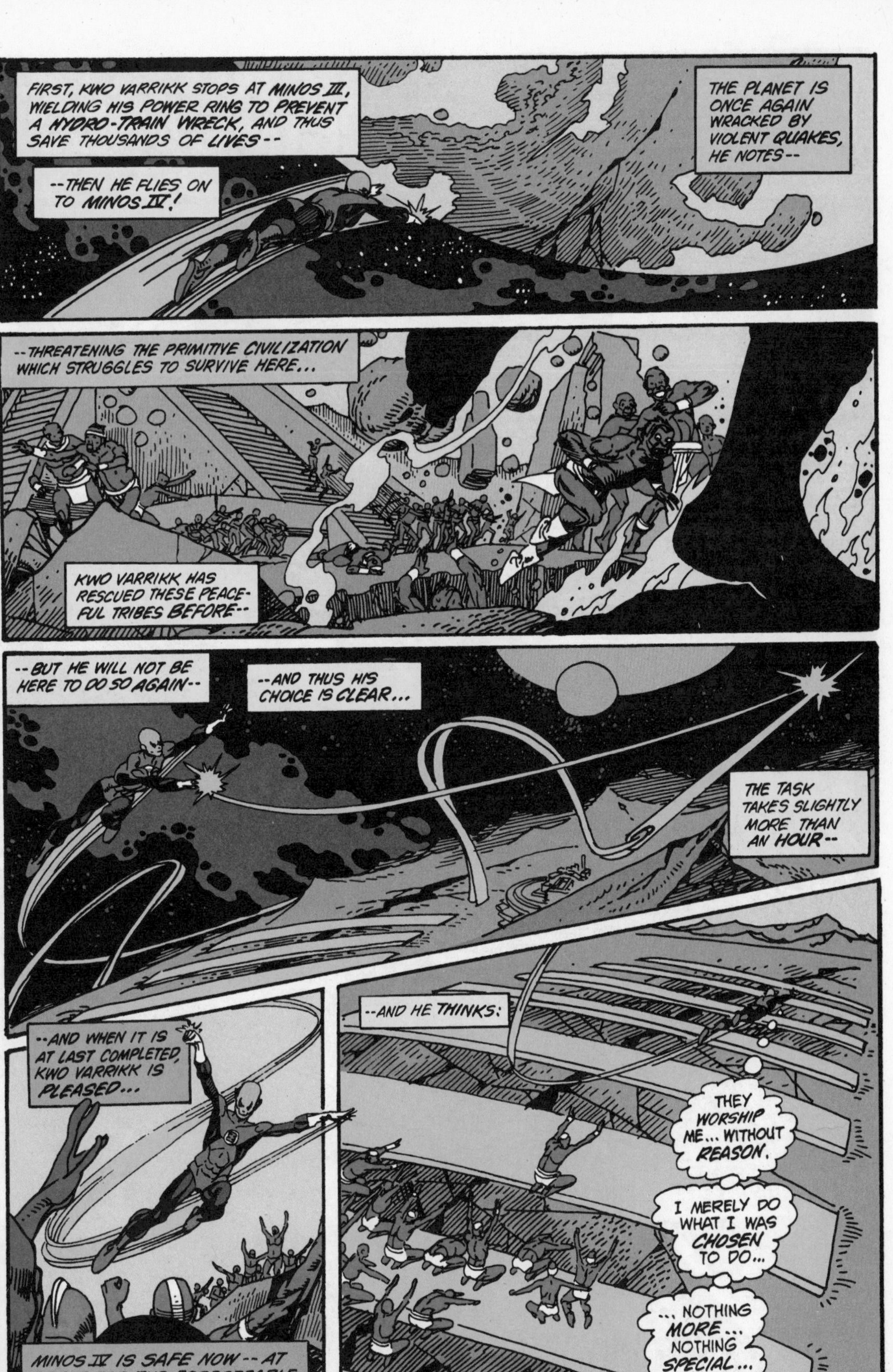
FIRST, KWO VARRIKK STOPS AT MINOS III, WIELDING HIS POWER RING TO PREVENT A HYDRO-TRAIN WRECK, AND THUS SAVE THOUSANDS OF LIVES--
--THEN HE FLIES ON TO MINOS IV!
THE PLANET IS ONCE AGAIN WRACKED BY VIOLENT QUAKES, HE NOTES--
--THREATENING THE PRIMITIVE CIVILIZATION WHICH STRUGGLES TO SURVIVE HERE...
KWO VARRIKK HAS RESCUED THESE PEACE-FUL TRIBES BEFORE--
--BUT HE WILL NOT BE HERE TO DO SO AGAIN--
--AND THUS HIS CHOICE IS CLEAR...
THE TASK TAKES SLIGHTLY MORE THAN AN HOUR--
--AND WHEN IT IS AT LAST COMPLETED, KWO VARRIKK IS PLEASED...
MINOS IV IS SAFE NOW--AT LEAST FOR THE FORESEEABLE FUTURE--
--AND HE THINKS:
THEY WORSHIP ME... WITHOUT REASON.
I MERELY DO WHAT I WAS CHOSEN TO DO...
...NOTHING MORE... NOTHING SPECIAL...

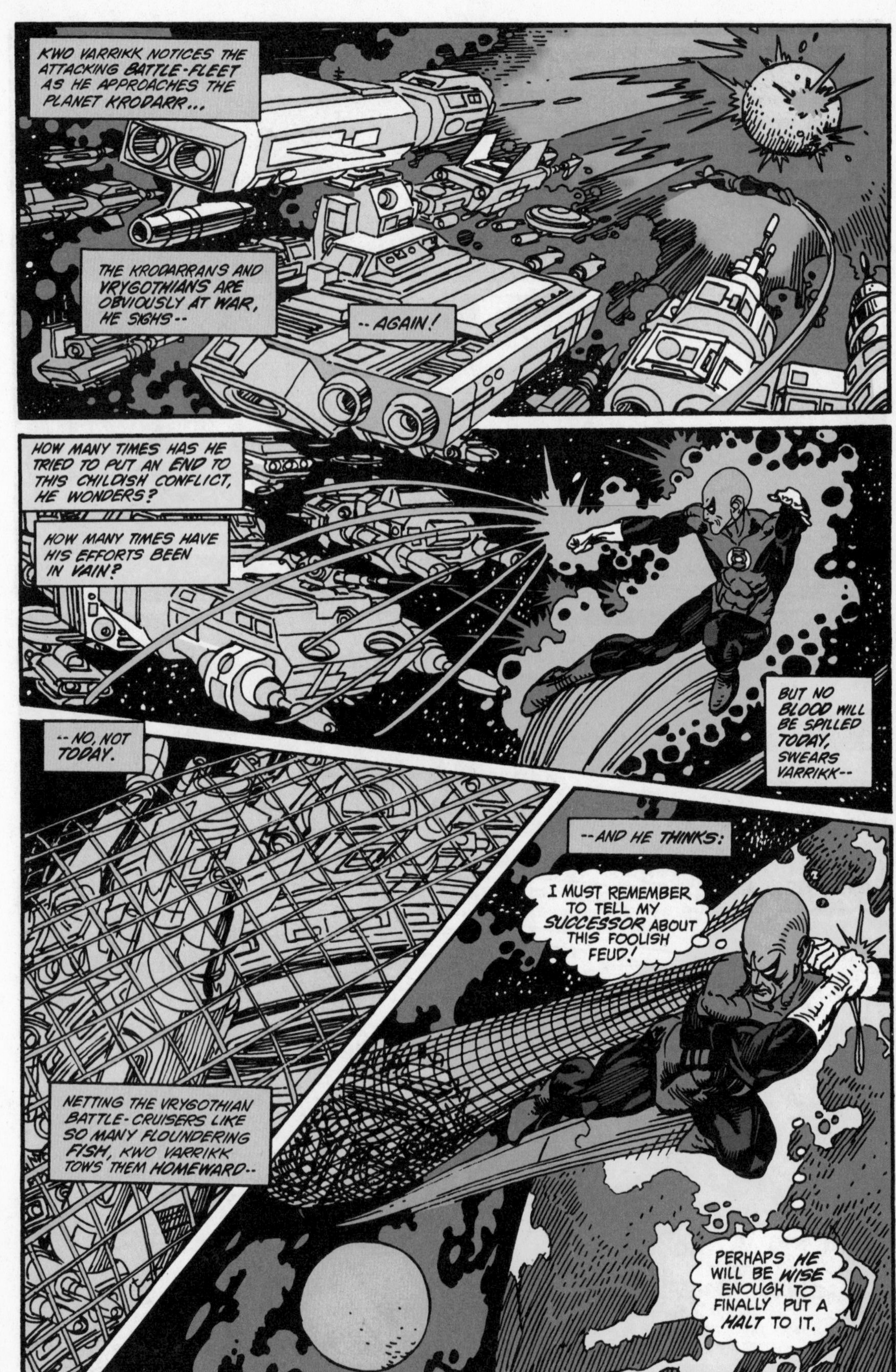
KWO VARRIKK NOTICES THE ATTACKING BATTLE-FLEET AS HE APPROACHES THE PLANET KRODARR...
THE KRODARRANS AND VRYGOTHIANS ARE OBVIOUSLY AT WAR, HE SIGHS--
--AGAIN!
HOW MANY TIMES HAS HE TRIED TO PUT AN END TO THIS CHILDISH CONFLICT, HE WONDERS?
HOW MANY TIMES HAVE HIS EFFORTS BEEN IN VAIN?
BUT NO BLOOD WILL BE SPILLED TODAY, SWEARS VARRIKK--
--NO, NOT TODAY.
--AND HE THINKS:
I MUST REMEMBER TO TELL MY SUCCESSOR ABOUT THIS FOOLISH FEUD!
NETTING THE VRYGOTHIAN BATTLE-CRUISERS LIKE SO MANY FLOUNDERING FISH, KWO VARRIKK TOWS THEM HOMEWARD--
PERHAPS HE WILL BE WISE ENOUGH TO FINALLY PUT A HALT TO IT.

LEAVING THE VRYGOTHIANS WITH A STERN (BUT HE FEARS FRUITLESS) WARNING, KWO VARRIKK FLIES ON--
--TO THE PLANET ONCE CALLED BLOODWORLD, NOW KNOWN AS ELYSIUM.
HERE, TWO HUNDRED YEARS BEFORE, KWO VARRIKK HAD FOUGHT AND DEFEATED THE DESPOTIC WARLORD K'RUNAK K'ANN -- AND BROUGHT PEACE TO THIS TROUBLED WORLD...
NOW KWO VARRIKK'S DEED IS REMEMBERED AS THE STUFF OF LEGEND, IF AT ALL--
--AND HIS JOURNEY HERE IS A MELANCHOLY MISSION AT BEST.
THERE IS NO NEED ON ELYSIUM NOW FOR THE POWER OF GREEN LANTERN--

--OR IS THERE?

VARRIKK SPIES AN OLD MAN PUFFING IN HOPELESS PURSUIT OF THE RUNAWAY PLAY-THING, A CHILD--OBVIOUSLY THE OWNER OF THE TOY--STRUGGLING TO KEEP PACE BEHIND HIM...

FOR AN INSTANT, KWO VARRIKK REMEMBERS HIS OWN YOUTH--
--NOW A THING OF DISTANT MEMORY.

THEN HE HANDS THE CHILD THE ELUSIVE KITE-STRING--
--AND HE THINKS:
I DID MY WORK WELL HERE ON ELYSIUM.
AYE--VERY WELL INDEED!

ON THE FINAL LEG OF HIS SECTOR-WIDE SOJOURN, KWO VARRIKK OBSERVES A MASSIVE METEOR-STORM STREAKING TOWARDS THE DENSELY-POPULATED PLANET CALLED BALGUS VI--
--AND USES THE AWESOME POWER OF HIS RING TO TURN THESE MIGHTY JUGGERNAUTS FROM THEIR PATH...
THIS COSMIC DEBRIS CAN BE PUT TO MUCH BETTER USE, HE DETERMINES--
--AS HE GUIDES THE HURTLING METEOROIDS ACROSS THE VOID TO A PLANET BARELY OUT OF ITS BIRTH THROES--
--WHERE HE PROTECTS THE STORM FROM THE DESTRUCTIVE FRICTION OF ATMOSPHERIC ENTRY--
--THEN DIRECTS THE MONSTROUS MASS INTO THE CHURNING HEART OF AN AZURE SEA--
--AND HE THINKS:
HOW INTRIGUING IT WOULD BE TO RETURN HERE ONE DAY--
--TO SEE WHAT MY SIMPLE EFFORTS HAVE WROUGHT!

AT LAST, KWO VARRIKK REACHES OA, GLEAMING JEWEL AT THE CENTER OF THE UNIVERSE, HOME OF THE IMMORTAL GUARDIANS--
--TO FIND HIS SUCCESSOR WAITING.
RETIREMENT IS NOT AN EASY THING FOR VARRIKK, BUT HE SURRENDERS HIS POWER RING GRACEFULLY--
--AND FEELS A TEAR COME TO HIS EYES AS HE WATCHES ANOTHER BEING RECEIVE THE AWESOME ENERGY THAT HAD BEEN HIS FOR SO MANY YEARS.
THEN THE CEREMONY IS OVER--
--AND HE KNOWS THE GUARDIANS HAVE ONCE AGAIN CHOSEN WELL.
SILENTLY, KWO VARRIKK TURNS TO LEAVE--
--AND A VOICE, QUITE LITERALLY OLDER THAN TIME, HALTS HIM IN HIS STEP.
IS KWO VARRIKK SATISFIED, THE GUARDIAN WONDERS?
HAVE HIS LONG YEARS OF SERVICE BEEN KIND TO HIM?
IS HE, AFTER ALL, TRULY HAPPY?
GENTLY, VARRIKK NODS--
--AND HE THINKS:
IT WAS A BEAUTIFUL KITE.
END

RIP
I, LANTERN
JOEY CAVALIERI WRITER
KEVIN O'NEILL ARTIST
JOHN COSTANZA LETTERER
ANTHONY TOLLIN COLORIST
LEN WEIN EDITOR
A FUNERAL?
THEY SHOULD CALL IT BY ITS RIGHT NAME... A TRAVESTY!
STEL RIP
GREEN LANTERN CORPS
YRON, PLEASE! THE OTHERS ARE STARING!
I DON'T CARE, ELGA! MOURNING IS USELESS--
--ESPECIALLY WHEN IT'S WASTED ON A FAILURE LIKE STEL!
HE WAS CHOSEN TO BE GREEN LANTERN OF THE PLANET GRENDA... AND WHAT DID HE ACCOMPLISH?
HE WAS NEVER ANY HELP AGAINST THE KRYDOS, AND FINALLY, HE MANAGED TO GET HIMSELF KILLED IN BATTLE!
THAT WAS HIS ONLY WORTHWHILE ACHIEVEMENT!
WHAT A TERRIBLE THING TO SAY! IT'S DISRESPECT!
IT WAS DISRESPECT FOR THE GUARDIANS TO PICK STEL TO BE GREEN LANTERN...
...AND NOT ME... THE MIGHTIEST OF ALL THE...
NO! THEY'RE BACK AGAIN! THE KRYDOS!

HOW CONVENIENT-- TO HAVE SO MANY OF THE BLASPHEMERS ALL IN ONE PLACE!
OPEN FIRE! I'LL REWARD THE MAN WHO SLAYS THE MOST!
DESTROY ALL THE MECHANICAL MEN! THEY ARE A PARODY OF LIFE-- AN AFFRONT TO THE CREATOR!
THEY DON'T DESERVE... EVEN A CLOCKWORK EXISTENCE!
WE'VE GOT TO GET OUT OF HERE! THEY WON'T BE HAPPY UNTIL WE'RE ALL BURNED-OUT HULLS!
YES-- HE'D ROLL OVER AND PLAY DEAD!
IF ONLY STEL WERE ALIVE! HE'D KNOW WHAT TO DO!
I INTEND TO STAY--
--AND FIGHT THEM!
I'LL SHOW THEM HOW I--
--WHAT? WHERE DID THAT COME FROM??

A GREEN LANTERN! OUR GREEN LANTERN, IT SEEMS!
THE GUARDIANS HAVE OBVIOUSLY PICKED STEL'S SUCCESSOR-- AN OFF-WORLDER!
WHA-- WHAT?
THEY SHOULD HAVE PICKED ME!
ME!
YOU'RE USELESS AGAINST THE KRYDOS... DON'T YOU SEE? PATHETIC!
SOMEONE SHOULD FIGHT THEM WHO KNOWS HOW...AND THAT SOMEONE IS ME!
TAKE ME TO OA... NOW...OR I'LL SNAP YOU LIKE A TWIG. YOU WON'T GET A CHANCE TO USE THAT RING!
I'M GOING TO FULFILL MY DESTINY! I'M GOING TO BECOME... A GREEN LANTERN!
YOU DO NOT FRIGHTEN ME, GRENDAN-- BUT FOR YOUR SAKE, I SHALL DO AS YOU SAY!

SHORTLY, AT THAT LEGENDARY WORLD AT THE VERY CENTER OF THE UNIVERSE...
AT LAST! THE GUARDIANS OF OA!
ARE YOU ALL ASSEMBLED? GOOD...I WON'T HAVE TO TROUBLE MYSELF BY REPEATING MY DEMAND!
I WANT--
WE KNOW WHAT YOU WANT!
THE GALAXY ECHOES WITH THE RINGING OF YOUR ARROGANT BELLOWING!
WHAT DO YOU THINK IS THE MEASURE OF A CORPSMAN--HOW LOUDLY HE THUMPS HIS CHEST AND WAILS?
IS THAT YOUR QUALIFICATION?
QUALIFICATION?
THIS IS MY QUALIFICATION!
OH, YOU WON'T FACE ME, EH?
WE'LL SEE NOW WHO WAILS AFTER I--
YOUR IRREVERENCE IS UNAMUSING, BUT DUE TO THE DIRE CIRCUMSTANCES OF YOUR PEOPLE, WE'LL ATTRIBUTE IT TO YOUR DISTRESS!
YET, WE... SYMPATHIZE WITH THE EMERGENCY ON YOUR PLANET! IF YOUR INDUCTION INTO THE CORPS WILL ALLEVIATE IT...
THEN, IN ALL GOOD CONSCIENCE-- WE MUST GRANT YOUR REQUEST!

I LIKE THE WHISTLING NOISE THEY MAKE WHEN THE SPHERES SAIL THROUGH THEM!
IS THAT ONE SUPPOSED TO BE A FEMALE? TRY CURLING UP WITH HER ON A COLD WINTER'S NIGHT! YOU'LL FREEZE YOUR TENDRILS!
ELGA! THE HEARTLESS VERMIN! THEY'RE TALKING ABOUT ELGA!
AIM FOR HER! LET'S SEE WHAT KIND OF NOISE SHE MAKES WHEN SHE SHATTERS!
I'VE GOT HER IN MY SIGHTS!
I'VE WAITED A LONG TIME FOR THIS! ELGA WILL REMAIN UN-HARMED, THANKS TO MY SUPERIOR INGENUITY!
THERE'S FAR TOO MANY OF THOSE SPHERES TO COLLECT, AND DEFLECTING THEM MIGHT DO WORSE DAMAGE IF THEY RICOCHET!
INSTEAD--
--THIS LOUDSPEAKER'S PITCH WILL SHATTER THE SPHERES--UNTIL THEY'RE NOTHING BUT--
EEEEEEEEEEEEEEEEEEEEEEEEEEEE

--DUST!?! NO! IT'S CLOGGING MY PEOPLE'S SYSTEMS-- ENTERING THEIR BRAINCASES-- THEIR JOINTS-- CHOKING OFF THEIR MOVEMENTS!

Y-Y-YRON!
ELGA!
BY THE GUARDIANS-- I--I'M KILLING HER!

I COUNTERED THEIR WEAPON--ONLY TO CREATE A WORSE ONE!
HOW COULD I HAVE DONE THIS? I'M A GREEN LANTERN! I'M A--

--FAILURE!

YRON OF GRENDA! YOU HAVE BRAGGED AND BULLIED YOUR WAY INTO THE GREEN LANTERN CORPS!
YOU HAVE DEFAMED THE MEMORY OF YOUR PREDECESSOR, STEL, WHO DIED VALIANTLY IN BATTLE! YOU PROCLAIMED FOR ALL YOUR COUNTRYMEN TO HEAR THAT STEL WAS ALWAYS USELESS AGAINST THE ON-SLAUGHT OF THE KRYDOS!
BUT NOW THAT YOU HAVE FACED YOUR RACE'S ENEMIES... YOUR EFFORTS PROVED FOOL-HARDY...AND DANGEROUS TO YOUR PEOPLE!
WE HAVE DONE AS YOU DEMANDED... NOW DO AS WE COMMAND...RETURN THE RING!
NEVER! I'M NOT A FAILURE! I WON'T LET YOU STRIP ME... OF WHAT I RIGHTFULLY DESERVE!
OF COURSE, BATTLING THE KRYDOS ON GRENDA ENDANGERED MY PEOPLE! LIVES ARE ALWAYS LOST IN WARFARE!
WOULD YOU BLAME THE KRYDOS' ATTACK ... ON ME?
JOEY CAVALIERI, WRITER
KEVIN O'NEILL, ARTIST
JOHN COSTANZA, LETTERER
ANTHONY TOLLIN, COLORIST
LEN WEIN, EDITOR
I, LANTERN PART TWO
TALES OF THE GREEN LANTERN CORPS
THEN, I WILL BRING THE WAR HERE... WHERE IT BELONGS...
...TO THE KRYDOS OUTPOST ITSELF!
I WILL STRIDE INTO THEIR STRONG-HOLD...AND DEMONSTRATE HOW A TRUE WARRIOR FACES AN ENEMY!
DON'T BELIEVE MY STATUS IN THE CORPS IS THE REASON FOR MY BRAVADO! IT'S AS EASY FOR ME TO HIDE MY NEW COLORS... AS IT IS TO DISPLAY THEM!

I HAD THIS LITTLE CLOCKWORK CREEP RIGHT IN MY SIGHTS! I SQUEEZED OFF ONE ROUND... THEN ANOTHER--
--NEXT THING YOU KNOW, THAT ROBOT'S PARTS WERE SPREAD ALL OVER THE SANDS!
HE TELLS THAT STORY OVER AND OVER AGAIN! I NEVER GET TIRED OF IT!
ONLY BECAUSE HE ADDS TO IT WITH EACH REPETITION!

DOES HE TELL THE PART ABOUT HOW HE WAS HUMILIATED BY A ROBOT?
I'M GETTING TO--WHAT?
WHAT ARE YOU TALKING ABOUT?
I'M TALKING ABOUT THE DISGRACE...THE DEFEAT YOU ALL WILL RECEIVE...

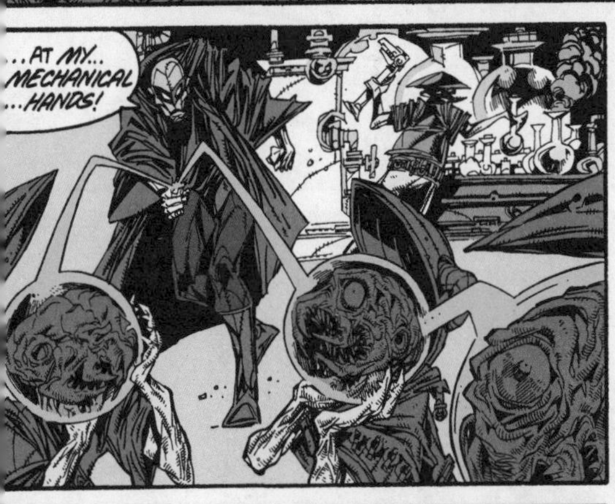
...AT MY... MECHANICAL ...HANDS!

BUT...NO! A VICTORY HERE IS A VICTORY IN A VACUUM!
FOR MY REVENGE TO BE SWEETER STILL...IT MUST BE WITNESSED.. BY MY FELLOW GRENDANS! THEY MUST SEE--

--HOW I BRAVELY DEAL WITH THE SCOURGE OF THEIR LIVES!
THEY WILL SEE... AND PROCLAIM ME... THEIR SAVIOR!

STEL
KRYDOS! SCATTER! THEY'LL KILL US ALL!
YRON BROUGHT THEM! HAS HE GONE MAD?

YOU ARE MAD INDEED, YRON! STEL WOULD NEVER PLACE THE LIVES OF HIS RACE IN JEOPARDY BY BRINGING HIS OWN WAR... HOME!
I TIRE OF THAT COMPARISON...I AM YRON...AND I AM THE GREEN LANTERN OF THIS SPACE SECTOR NOW...ITS SWIFT AND MERCILESS WEAPON AGAINST THE KRYDOS!
A WEAPON THAT CANNOT BE WIELDED--

--WHILE IT IS IN ITS DEATH THROES!
KRSSSSSHH

WE PLANNED TO DROP BOMBS OF THIS CORROSIVE ON YOUR PLANET... FINALLY WIPING OUT YOUR ARTIFICIAL MOCKERY OF LIFE!
I AM GLAD TO SEE THAT.. IT IS EFFECTIVE!

THIS GREEN LANTERN DID US A GOOD TURN! HE PROVIDED US WITH GRAND DIVERSION!
AND WE DIDN'T EVEN HAVE TO EXPEND THE ENERGY FOR THE TRIP!

THEY'RE GOING TO GO ON... TO MASSACRE MY PEOPLE... AGAIN... AND IT'S ALL MY FAULT!
THE GUARDIANS... THE WERE... RIGHT! STEL... WHATEVER HIS FAULTS... NEVER BROUGHT SUCH IGNOMINY... SUCH TRAGEDY... ON HIS OWN KIND!
STEL
RIP

STEL...HAD JUDGMENT... DISCRETION... HE WAS VALIANT...KNEW WHEN TO FIGHT... AND WHEN TO WALK AWAY FROM A FIGHT!
MY PEOPLE DON'T NEED ME...THEY NEED STEL!

STEL!
STEL

THE LAST GASP... THE LAST SIGH OF RELEASE OF ONE WHO GIVES UP HIS LIFE... FOR HIS PEOPLE...
...COALESCES... INTO ONE LAST SURGE OF WILL POWER... ONE FINAL SUMMONING OF DETERMINATION...
STEL
RIP

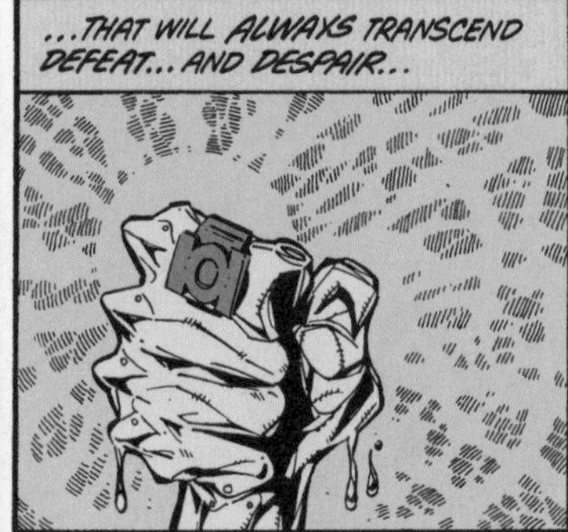

...THAT WILL ALWAYS TRANSCEND DEFEAT... AND DESPAIR...

THAT WILL PERHAPS TRANSCEND EVEN... DEATH!
RIP

EVERY RACE... EVERY RELIGION... BELIEVES THAT IN ITS HOUR OF MOST DIRE NEED... THERE WILL COME A SAVIOR.

THAT SAVIOR HAS COME.

THAT SAVIOR IS STEL--

--GREEN LANTERN... OF GRENDA!

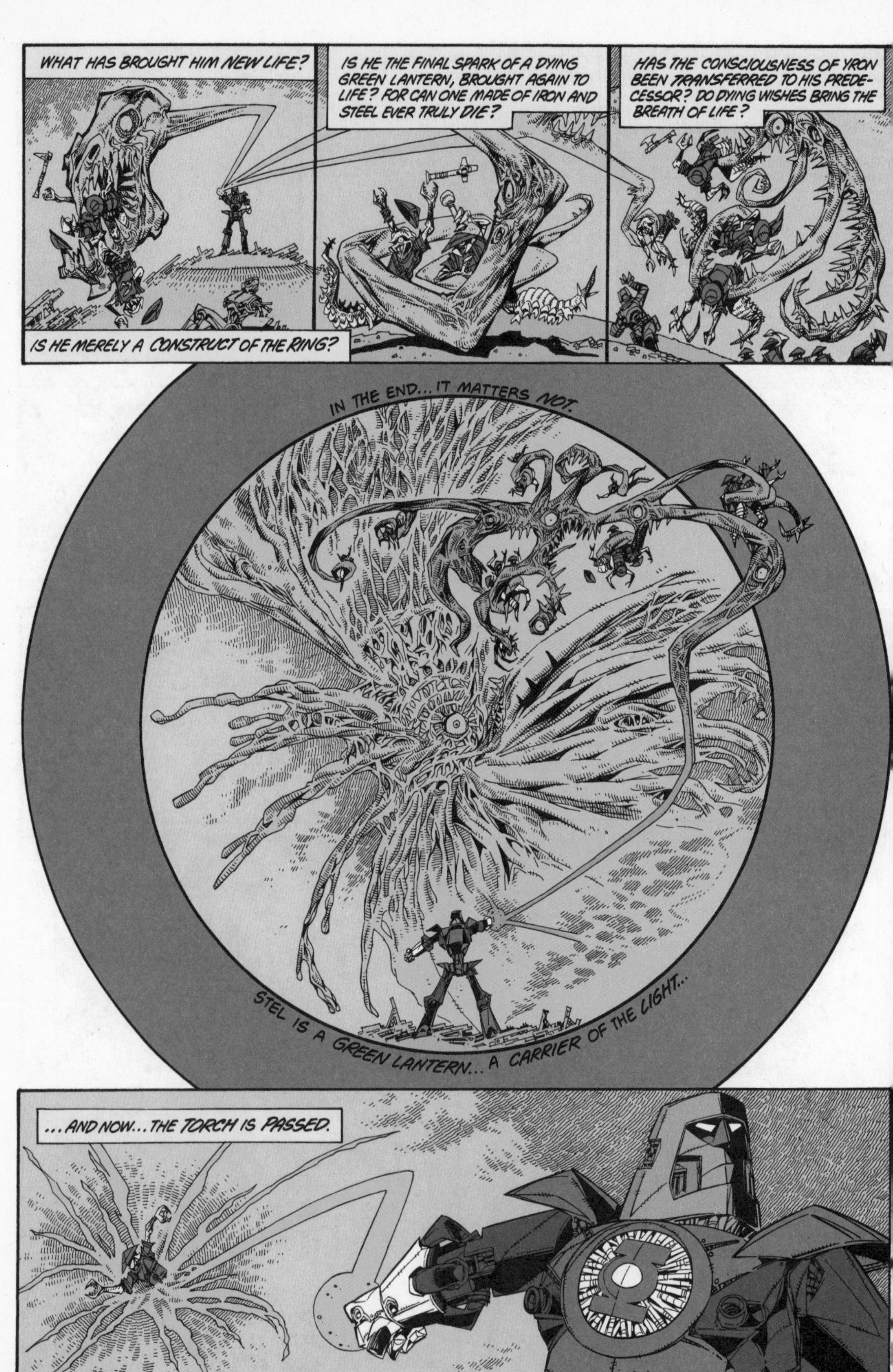
WHAT HAS BROUGHT HIM NEW LIFE?
IS HE THE FINAL SPARK OF A DYING GREEN LANTERN, BROUGHT AGAIN TO LIFE? FOR CAN ONE MADE OF IRON AND STEEL EVER TRULY DIE?
HAS THE CONSCIOUSNESS OF YRON BEEN TRANSFERRED TO HIS PREDECESSOR? DO DYING WISHES BRING THE BREATH OF LIFE?
IS HE MERELY A CONSTRUCT OF THE RING?
IN THE END... IT MATTERS NOT.
STEL IS A GREEN LANTERN... A CARRIER OF THE LIGHT...
...AND NOW... THE TORCH IS PASSED.

STEL! YOU'VE COME BACK TO US! YOU'RE OUR GREEN LANTERN AGAIN!
IT'S ABOUT TIME! YRON WAS DREADFUL! HE--

DO NOT SEEK TO BLAME HIM.
BREATHES THERE A LIVING BEING WITH SOUL SO DEAD.. THAT HE CAN STAND BY AND WATCH HIS COUNTRYMEN CRINGE AND COWER IN FEAR OF THEIR ENEMIES?

DO NOT TELL ME OF HIS FAULTS. TELL ME OF HIS ACTIONS.
HE SAW HIS NATION UNDER SIEGE. HE ROSE TO DEFEND IT. THAT MAKES HIM A HERO.

HE KNEW HE COULD NOT DEFEAT OUR ENEMIES... SO HE GAVE HIS ALL... TO RESTORE LIFE TO SOMEONE WHO COULD.
THAT MAKES HIM YOUR SAVIOR.

REMEMBER HIM WELL... AND WHEN THE TIME COMES...

HOPE THAT YOU MAY BE VALIANT ENOUGH... TO DO THE SAME.

RIP

YRON

"DE MORTUUIS, NIL NISI BONUM."

END

WHAT PRICE HONOR?
HIARAAA!
RUBEN DIAZ-WRITER
TRAVIS CHAREST-PENCILLER
RAY McCARTHY
AGOP GEMDJIAN -INKERS
BOB LAPPAN-LETTERERERER
STEVE MATTSSON-COLORIST

TE AN INTERESTING PUPIL YOU HAVE THERE.
WHO IS SHE?
HER NAME IS LAIRA. SHE'S THE DAUGHTER OF KENTOR OMOTO, THE PREVIOUS GREEN LANTERN OF SECTOR 112.

KRACK


SWOOF

SHE HAS THE GRACE OF AN EARTH FAWN.
YES, ND THE FEROCITY JF A KAROZIAN SKY-SHARK!

AFTER THE INCIDENT WITH KENTOR, DO YOU THINK SHE HOLDS ANY RESENTMENT TOWARDS THE CORPS?

AS FAR BACK AS I CAN REMEMBER, I LONGED TO BE A GREEN LANTERN. SO STRONG WAS MY DESIRE THAT MY FATHER PRIMED ME TO BE HIS SUCCESSOR.

I THOUGHT MY WORLD WOULD CRUMBLE WHEN HE LEFT. HE TOLD ME HE WAS NEEDED TO FIGHT A COSMIC CRISIS. I FEARED HE WOULD NEVER RETURN.

MY FEARS CAME TRUE. CYCLES PASSED BEFORE THE GUARDIANS APPEARED WITH THE DREADFUL NEWS. MY FATHER WAS GONE AND I WAS CONSIDERED TO TAKE HIS PLACE. I MADE A VOW...

STOP!
...NOTHING WILL STOP ME
FROM BEING A GREEN LANTERN!
OHH! I'M... SORRY.
THAT'S FINE, LAIRA. REMEMBER TO FOCUS YOUR POWER TO CONCENTRATE, BUT NOT TO GIVE IN TO EMOTION.
END THE SESSION AND MEET ME IN THE ANTECHAMBER.
YES, SIR.
DO YOU THINK IT WISE SEND HER BACK SOON? SHE IS MUCH TOO CRUDE.
WELL, HE HAS NO CHOICE. RISK OF SOUNDING CHÉD, IT MUST BE HER APTISM BY FIRE."
YOU HAVE PERFORMED EXCELLENTLY, LAIRA. WE HAVE DECIDED THAT YOUR TRAINING IS REACHING COMPLETION.
THIS COULD NOT HAVE HAPPENED AT A BETTER MOMENT. THERE IS A CRISIS ON YOUR HOME-WORLD, LAIRA...
BUT I'M SURE YOU ARE AWARE OF WHAT SHE'S FACING.
TRUST ME.

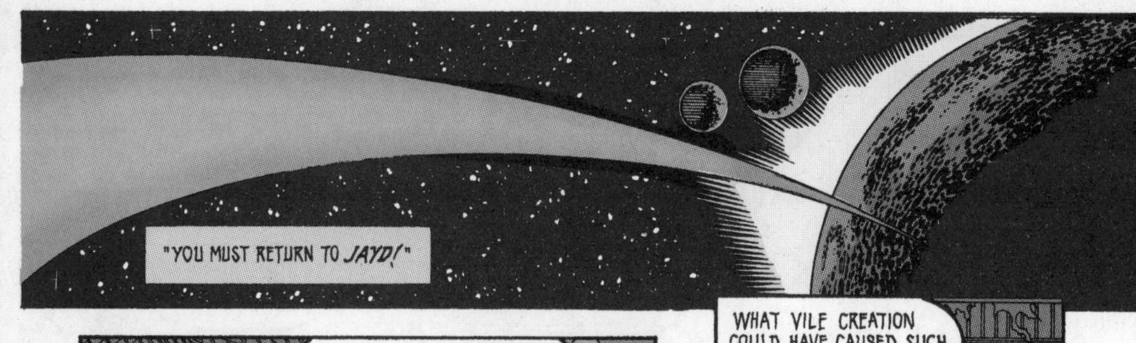
"YOU MUST RETURN TO *JAYD!*"

*BY ÇÏVA,* THIS CANNOT BE THE X'OL I REMEMBER! "THE CITY OF BRIGHT TOMORROWS" LAID WASTE BEFORE ME...!

WHAT VILE CREATION COULD HAVE CAUSED SUCH DEVASTATION?
THE *MOST* VILE...
HUH?

IT WAS A BEAST OF *FLESH AND BLOOD* THAT LED X'OL TO ROT. THAT TERRIBLE OGRE WHO TOOK THE SHAPE OF MAN TERRORIZED US... ALL IN THE REMAKING OF X'OL IN HIS IMAGE.
WHERE IS THIS MADMAN?

THERE! THAT HELLISH CASTLE IS THE HOME OF...

"THE GOLDEN DRAGON."

A PITY, THE PRICE TO BE PAID FOR TRADITION. SINCE MY DISSOLUTION OF THAT INCOMPETENT DRÆZ COUNCIL, X'OL HAS REJECTED MY BENEVOLENCE.

IT IS JUST OBVIOUS PEOPLE DO NOT RECOGNIZE WHAT'S GOOD FOR THEM.

PARDONS, MY PATRON. WORD HAS COME THAT A GREEN LANTERN IS IN X'OL.
INDEED. THEN, ALERT THE ELITE GUARD AND BRING MY ARMOR.

MY LIEGE--!

THE TIME HAS COME, THEN, AS I KNEW IT WOULD. DESTINY CAN NEVER BE MAN'S CHOICE.
IT MUST BE HER WHO COMES TO OPPOSE ME.

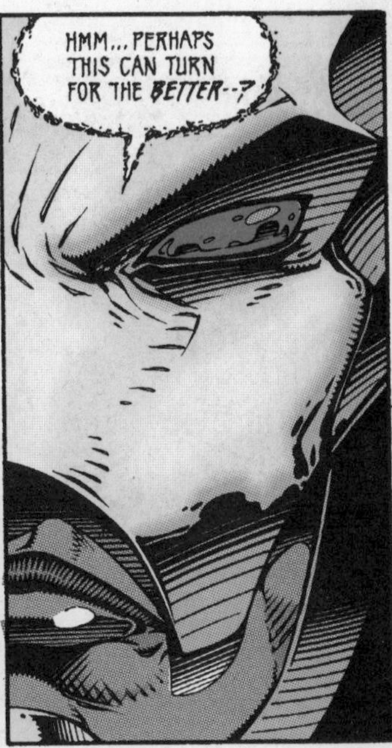
HMM... PERHAPS THIS CAN TURN FOR THE BETTER--?

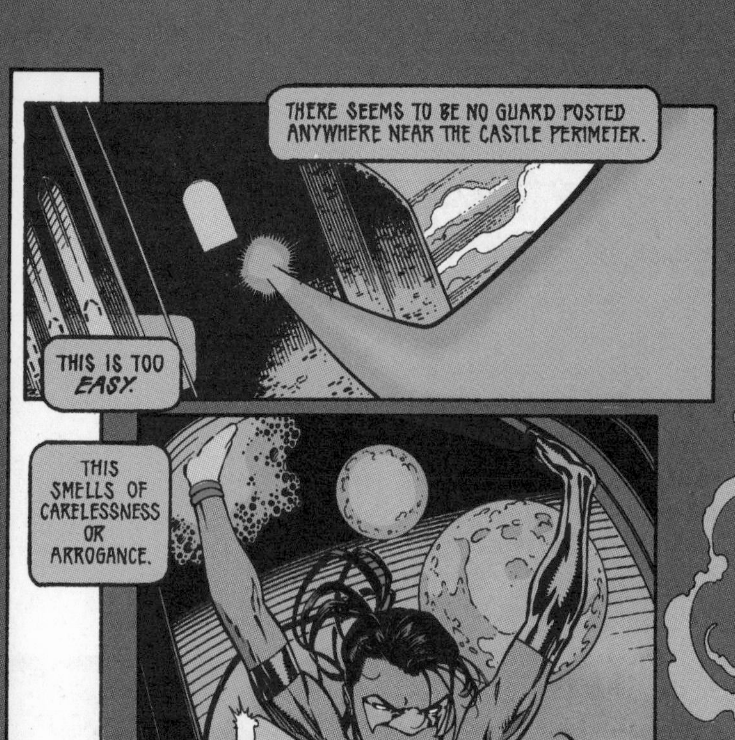
THERE SEEMS TO BE NO GUARD POSTED ANYWHERE NEAR THE CASTLE PERIMETER.
THIS IS TOO *EASY.*
THIS SMELLS OF CARELESSNESS OR ARROGANCE.

I'M GLAD I TRAINED ON OA. MY FATHER NEVER PREPARED ME FOR ANYTHING LIKE *THIS.*

I HAVE TO BE CAREFUL NOT TO CREATE ENOUGH LIGHT THAT I'D BE--

--*DISCOVERED!*

HOW STUPID COULD I HAVE BEEN?
HRAA111-AH
BACK ON OA, EVEN THE BEST CADET COULD NEVER SNEAK UP ON ME.
COULD IT BE I WAS JUST THE *BEST OF THE WORST?*

UNGH!
MAYBE I *WASN'T* PREPARED.

IT SEEMS ALL OF MY LIFE, MY CHOICES HAVE BEEN DICTATED BY SOMEONE ELSE.
BUT THE TIME TO PONDER THAT HAS LONG PASSED.

I'M TOO INVOLVED IN THIS TO QUIT NOW.

EITHER I FIND FAITH IN MY *ABILITIES* OR NOT ONLY IS ALL OF JAYD DOOMED...

...BUT SO AM I.

THAT'S THE CREST I SAW STREWN THROUGHOUT X'OL!
MY HEART IS POUNDING SO MUCH I CAN HARDLY THINK.

CAN'T BECOME COCKY. I CAN'T EXPECT THESE GUARDS TO BE AS EASY AS THE OTHERS.
AEIIII

I MUST CONCENTRATE. REMEMBER THE TRAINING ARENAS.

BUT NOW IT'S BRUTALLY REAL!

AND MORE THAN MERIT IS DEPENDENT ON MY SUCCESS.

NOW IS THE CHANCE TO PROVE MYSELF TRUE TO THE MEMORY OF MY FATHER...
...BUT ABOVE ALL ELSE, THAT I'M WORTHY OF BEING A GREEN LANTERN.

COME IN, EMERALD WARRIOR.
I KNEW YOU WERE COMING!
THEN FACE ME, COWARD.
COWARD? HARDLY.
IS THIS ANY WAY TO TREAT YOUR HOST?
COME TO END YOUR REIGN OF TERROR
D GIVE X'OL BACK TO ITS PEOPLE... EVEN
F IT TAKES TILL MY DYING BREATH!
NOW FACE ME
LESS YOU FEAR ME!
CONCENTRATE... REMAIN FOCUSED... DON'T GIVE IN TO EMOTIONS...
THE GOLDEN DRAGON FEARS TO LOOK INTO THE EYES OF NO ONE!
YOU SHOULD CALL ME MASTER!

WHY DO YOU OPPOSE ME? I AM MERELY ACTING IN X'OL'S BEST INTEREST.
SINCE WHEN IS SUPPRESSION AND DESTRUCTION IN X'OL'S INTEREST?
SSSSSS

SSSZZZT
I AM JUST STRUGGLING TO PRESERVE HER TIME-HONORED CUSTOMS.

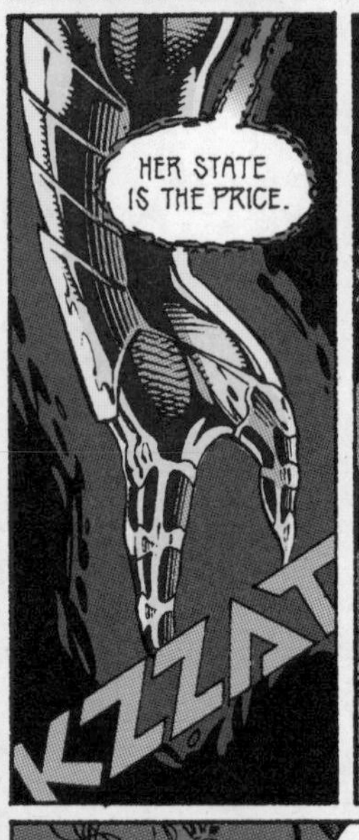
HER STATE IS THE PRICE.
KZZZAT

CAN'T YOU SEE YOUR COMPULSION IS KILLING THESE PEOPLE?
WERE YOU NOT RAISED ON HONOR AND TRADITION?
YES, BUT--
HE MUST HAVE RECOGNIZED ME AS A JAYDIAN.

YES, BUT YOU GIVE *THEM* NO CHOICE!

HAS YOUR NEW ALLEGIANCE CAUSED YOU TO BECOME *BLIND*?

CAN HE BE RIGHT? AM I SUBCONSCIOUSLY ALLOWING DEFEAT?

WOULD YOU NOT DIE FOR THAT?
YOUR EMERALD WEAPONS ARE USELESS! YOU WASTE YOUR TIME!
THEN LET'S END THIS QUICKLY.
WOCK
ARRRRG!
ÇIVA'S BLOOD!

DID I NOT TEACH YOU WELL, DAUGHTER?
YOU CAN'T BE MY FATHER. KENTOR OMOTO FOUGHT FOR THE GOOD OF JAYD!
BUT I STILL AM!
I LABORED MANY SEASONS FOR THE RESTORATION OF A GREAT HISTORY. I WOULD ONLY ALLOW MY KIN TO SUCCEED ME.
NEVER!
BUT YOU WOULD AS A GREEN LANTERN?
THAT SELF-RIGHTEOUS CLIQUE IS MORE IMPORTANT THAN YOUR COUNTRY'S HONOR?
BUT I SAW YOU LEAV
I WAS TOLD YOU WER
DEAD. HOW CAN YOU
MY FATHER?
IF YOU ARE, CAN I DEFEAT THE MAN I VOWED TO EMULAT

AS GREEN LANTERN OF SECTOR 112 AND A NATIVE F JAYD, I RESENTED THE RÆZ COUNCIL'S DECISION O SLOWLY ABOLISH IMELESS RULES.
THEY SOUGHT TO BE "PROGRESSIVE," BUT THIS WAS SACRILEGIOUS! WHILE I FOUGHT PERILS IN SPACE, MY HOME-WORLD BECAME A STRANGE PLACE.
ONE DAY I RETURNED TO SEE PUBLIC CAVORTING AND WANTON, LEWD BEHAVIOR. X'OL BECAME *DEMORALIZED* AND I WOULD NOT STAND FOR IT!
SED MY RING TO INFLUENCE THE COUNCIL RESCIND THEIR EDICTS. I TRIED TO RESTORE NOR. IT WORKED TIL THE *GUARD-S* DISCOVERED PLAN.
THOSE *POMPOUS DWARVES* CHARGED ME WITH POLITICAL INTERFERENCE! I WAS *STRIPPED* OF MY GREEN LANTERN DUTY AND RELEASED TO THE CUSTODY OF THE COUNCIL.
IN TURN, THE COUNCIL DECIDED TO *BANISH* ME.
BANISHED, I LOCATED A SMALL CULT THAT WORSHIPPED ME WHEN I WAS A G.L. THEY HELPED CREATE THE GOLDEN DRAGON. SINCE THEN, I VOWED TO RESTORE JAYD'S PURITY WITHOUT THE HELP OF THAT INFERNAL RING!

I DO BELIEVE IN THE BETTERMENT OF X'OL. BUT, I PREFER THE METHODS OF THE GREEN LANTERNS TO YOURS!
MY ALLEGIANCE IS NOW TO THEM.
THAT PLEDGE CALLS TO DEFEAT ANY OPPRESSION OF MY SECTOR!
THEN YOU LEAVE ME NO CHOICE!
THWOK
THADUNK
HE IS NO LONGER THE FATHER I KNEW. I MUST AT LEAST STAY TRUE TO THE CORPS.
I'VE TRIED EVERYTHING WITHIN MY TRAINING TO STOP HIM. AND I STILL CAN'T GET BEYOND THE EMOTION. WAIT...
HA HA HA HA
FORGIVE ME, FATHER!
SCRAWK

YOU'VE BESTED ME. I WOULD RATHER DIE THAN LIVE WITH THIS DISGRACE.
HONOR ME; KILL ME!
SWIP
-KOFF- FINISH ME!
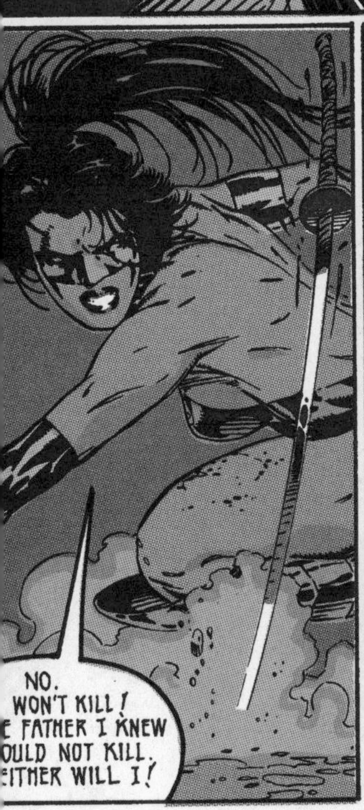
NO. WON'T KILL! E FATHER I KNEW OULD NOT KILL. EITHER WILL I!

AS I SEE IT, YOU ARE ALREADY FINISHED!
IF YOU SEEK AN END, FINISH YOURSELF.
LAIRA...

SSSSSSSSKT

GUARDIANS, I SUMMON YOU.

YES, LAIRA. WE HAVE BEEN MONITORING YOUR PROGRESS AND WE'RE PLEASED.

I DON'T CARE FOR YOUR *GRACES.* WHY WASN'T I TOLD THE COMPLETE TRUTH ABOUT MY FATHER AND THIS MISSION?!

IT WOULD HAVE CLOUDED YOUR JUDGMENTS ON THIS ASSIGNMENT AS A *GREEN LANTERN.*

WE NEEDED TO ASSURE YOU WERE WITHOUT FEAR. WHAT BETTER WAY THAN TO *CONFRONT* IT?

BESIDES, WE KNEW THIS EXERCISE WOULD BE AN EXCELLENT WAY TO JUDGE YOUR SKILLS AND *LOYALTY.*

I'M SURE THAT HAS BEEN PROVEN.

BUT I WILL NOT SUPPORT LIES OR DECEPTION AGAIN. THEY HAVE ALREADY BROUGHT ME GREAT LOSS... *TWICE!*

WELL, WITH YOUR TRAINING COMPLETED, WE CONSIDERED RELOCATING YOU TO ANOTHER SECTOR...
NO. THAT WILL NOT HAPPEN.
I'M NEEDED HERE.
...BUT WE FIGURED THAT.
THE END?

# DECENT EXPOSURE

**Writer:** TODD KLEIN **Penciller:** JOE STATON **Inker:** BRUCE PATTERSON

# MOGO DOESN'T SOCIALZE

**Writer:** ALAN MOORE **Artist:** DAVE GIBBONS

Originally presented in GREEN LANTERN No. 188, May 1985

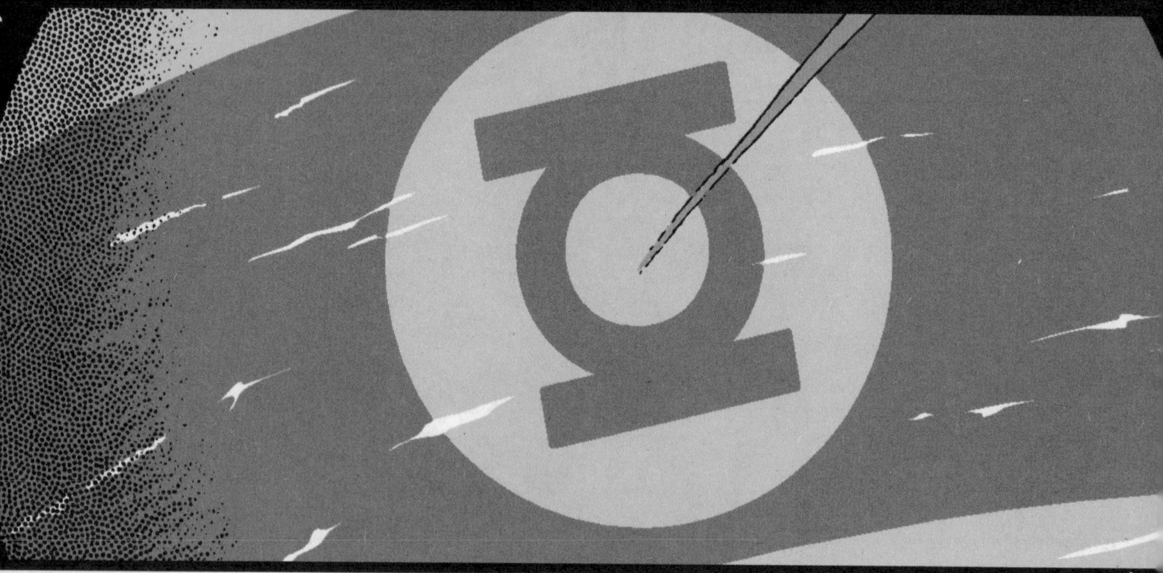

GREEN LANTERN #188 marked many things. It was Steve Englehart and Joe Staton's first issue together. They would continue on the book, eventually transforming it into GREEN LANTERN CORPS with issue #201. This period was a definite high point for both DC with the revamping of its universe during CRISIS ON INFINITE EARTHS and for GREEN LANTERN itself. Steve and Joe weaved together one of the very best runs the character has ever seen.

GREEN LANTERN #188 was also the first time John Stewart, as the newly appointed Green Lantern, revealed his identity to the public. It was before its time, before secret identities were compromised, and it immediately defined John Stewart for who he was. A hero who wanted to be trusted and a hero who wasn't afraid to get his hands dirty.

GREEN LANTERN #188 was also the first appearance of Mogo. The planet-sized Green Lantern created by Alan Moore and Dave Gibbons. Mogo was one of the most intriguing creations ever to be born from the GREEN LANTERN title. Mogo has since become a major element in the Green Lantern mythos. Rookies and veterans alike make pilgrimage to Mogo to face their greatest fears. The landscape literally changes around an officer. In addition, Mogo acts as the compass of sorts that guides the power rings to their bearers. Without Mogo, the rings would be directionless when searching for a replacement.

Finally, GREEN LANTERN #188 marked the very first GREEN LANTERN issue I ever purchased. A helluva issue to stumble on, I think. Between the start of Englehart and Staton's run, the shock of seeing someone other than Hal Jordan wearing the ring, John Stewart revealing his identity to the world and the introduction to the "biggest" Green Lantern ever, this remains one of the key issues in the Green Lantern universe.

– Geoff Johns

CONTINUING--A RICH HERITAGE BEGUN MANY YEARS AGO BY JULIE SCHWARTZ, JOHN BROOME, GIL KANE, AND GARDNER FOX--
--TOUCHED FOREVER BY DENNY O'NEIL AND NEAL ADAMS--
--AND HANDED A SURPRISING NEW TWIST TONIGHT BY--
TAWNY YOUNG, K-LAQ 'ON THE SPOT' NEWS! THIS REPORTER HAS LEARNED EXCLUSIVELY THAT THE NEW
GREEN LANTERN®
IS AN ARCHITECT FROM DETROIT NAMED JOHN STEWART--
--CURRENTLY EMPLOYED BY FERRIS AIRCRAFT HERE IN THE L.A. AREA!
SAY WHA-AT--?!!
DECENT EXPOSURE
STEVE ENGLEHART - WRITER ☼ JOE STATON - PENCILLER ☼ BRUCE PATTERSON - INKER
HELEN VESIK - LETTERER ☼ TONY TOLLIN - COLORIST ☼ ANDY HELFER - EDITOR

"STEWART FIRST APPEARED SEVERAL YEARS AGO, WHEN HE HELPED THE FIRST GREEN LANTERN EXPOSE THE RACIST SCHEMES OF PRESIDENTIAL CANDIDATE SENATOR JEREMIAH CLUTCHER--

"--AND EXPOSED HIS FACE FOR ALL THE WORLD TO SEE!
"UNFORTUNATELY, HE WAS MOVING SO FAST THAT NO ONE GOT A CLEAR PICTURE OF HIM, AND AFTER THAT ONE NIGHT, HE VANISHED!

"SINCE THEN, HE'S BEEN REPORTED ON THE AVERAGE OF ONCE A YEAR--UNMASKED--EVERYWHERE FROM ST. LOUIS TO STAR CITY--
"--BUT ALWAYS, HE WAS GONE BEFORE THE NEWS CREWS COULD ARRIVE!"

THE FIRST GREEN LANTERN, WHILE AFFIRMING HIS FAITH IN HIS PHANTOM PARTNER, WOULD NEVER DISCUSS HIM, AND THE SECOND G.L. SEEMED, AT BEST, A SIDEBAR, WHILE THE FIRST G.L. CONTINUED HIS CAREER!

HOWEVER, WHEN THE PARTNER--NOW MASKED FOR THE FIRST TIME--TOLD ME EXCLUSIVELY LAST MONDAY THAT HE HAD REPLACED THE FIRST G.L., I BEGAN AN INTENSIVE INVESTIGATION --AND FOUND, TO MY COMPLETE SURPRISE--

"--ANY NUMBER OF PEOPLE WHO KNEW HIS IDENTITY!"
YEAH, THAT'S HIM! HE REBUILT OUR WHOLE NEIGHBORHOOD ONE CHRISTMAS!
RICHIE SAYS HIS NAME'S JOHN STEWART--BUT I'M NOT S'POSED TO TELL!

JOHN AND I WERE, UH, HAVING DINNER ONE NIGHT, WHEN THIS GREEN GLOW FILLED THE ROOM! IT ALL BUT BLINDED ME--
--BUT I SAW HIM TURN INTO GREEN LANTERN! YOU BET I DID!

JOHN'S MY ONLY SON, MISS YOUNG.
I'M AFRAID I HAVE NO COMMENT--
--EXCEPT TO SAY THAT I'VE ALWAYS BEEN VERY PROUD OF HIM!

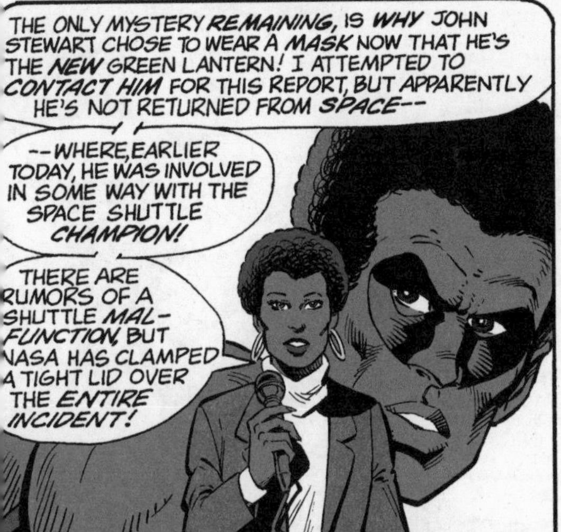
THE ONLY MYSTERY REMAINING, IS WHY JOHN STEWART CHOSE TO WEAR A MASK NOW THAT HE'S THE NEW GREEN LANTERN! I ATTEMPTED TO CONTACT HIM FOR THIS REPORT, BUT APPARENTLY HE'S NOT RETURNED FROM SPACE--
--WHERE, EARLIER TODAY, HE WAS INVOLVED IN SOME WAY WITH THE SPACE SHUTTLE CHAMPION!
THERE ARE RUMORS OF A SHUTTLE MAL-FUNCTION, BUT NASA HAS CLAMPED A TIGHT LID OVER THE ENTIRE INCIDENT!

"I DID, HOWEVER, SPEAK WITH SUPERMAN AND GREEN ARROW--"
HE'S A GOOD MAN-- A BRAVE MAN --!
ABSOLUTELY!

--SO, IN CONCLUSION, WE MAY BE SURE THAT JOHN STEWART, THE NEW GREEN LANTERN, WILL CONTINUE TO BE A HOT STORY FOR MANY MONTHS TO COME!
WE MAY NEVER KNOW WHAT HAPPENED TO THE OLD G.L., BUT THE NEW ONE LOOKS TO BE JUST AS GOOD, IF NOT BETTER--

FUNNY THING, TELEVISION! NOTHING ELSE TOUCHES SO MANY PEOPLE SO DIRECTLY, AND ALL AT THE SAME TIME...
CLIK!

IN MALIBU--
WOW!
HAL--?
IT'S ALL RIGHT, CAROL! I WAS JUST WONDERING WHAT I'D HAVE DONE IF THEY'D ANNOUNCED MY SECRET IDENTITY ON THE TUBE!
ALL THE TROUBLE I WENT THROUGH TO KEEP THAT SECRET--TRUSTING ONLY YOU AND TOM* IN THE NON-SUPER WORLD FOR ALL THOSE YEARS--!
BUT SHE'S RIGHT! JOHN'S NEVER CARED!
*KALMAKU, HAL'S RIGHT-HAND MAN. --A.

WELL, THAT'S ALLOWED YOU TO RETIRE--AND HE NEVER CAN, NOW!
BUT, HAL, HOW COME I DIDN'T KNOW ABOUT HIM? JOHN WORKS FOR ME, AT YOUR RECOMMENDATION!
YOU HEARD THE LADY! I DON'T DISCUSS OTHER PEOPLE'S SECRETS--NOT EVEN WITH THE WOMAN I LOVE!

I WOULD THINK, THOUGH, THAT AFTER ALL THE TROUBLE I HAD WITH ONE GREEN LANTERN--
WAIT! FORGET I SAID THAT! I DON'T WANT TO ARGUE WITH YOU AGAIN!
DOESN'T MATTER! ITS TAKEN ME SOME TIME TO GET COMFORTABLE WITH THE CHANGES WE'VE MADE--THERE'S NO REASON TO EXPECT YOU, TO BE DIFFERENT!
SORRY I'M SO HARD TO PLEASE THESE DAYS--I DON'T WANT TO BE--!
BUT WE'VE GOT TO LOOK TO THE FUTURE FROM NOW ON! THERE'S ONLY ONE PROBLEM WE STILL HAVE TO SOLVE, AND--
RRINNG!

HELLO--?
YES, HE'S HERE--!

HELLO--?
THAT CRAZY WOMAN! SHE NEVER TOLD US SHE WAS GONNA REVEAL JOHN'S IDENTITY! SHE JUST ASKED WHAT WE THOUGHT OF HIM! I SHOULDA KNOWN SHE WAS TOO WIDE-EYED, TOO SWEET--!

STAR CITY--
HI, ARROW!
HI, YOURSELF! YOU'RE LUCKY IT NEVER HAPPENED TO YOU--THE "OLD G.L."! HOW'S IT FEEL, WATCHIN' YOUR OWN WAKE?
IT--UH--DOESN'T BOTHER ME IN THE LEAST, G.A.!

I MADE THE RIGHT DECISION!
WELL, GOOD! I THINK SO, TOO!
WELL, I JUST WANTED TO CHECK IN, BUDDY! GOT A BAD GUY TO ROUND UP! WE'LL SEE YA SOON!
TAKE CARE!
YOU TOO! KISS THE CANARY FOR ME!

I KNEW IT, DINAH! HE'S NEVER HAPPY UNLESS HE THINKS HE'S SCREWED UP!
AND IT'S THAT DAMNED CAROL FERRIS WHO'S DONE IT TO HIM!

I'M TURNING ON THE ANSWERING MACHINE! IT'LL ONLY BE MEDIA FOR THE REST OF THE NIGHT!
GOOD IDEA! I WANT TO CONCENTRATE ON OUR REAL CONCERN--THE IDENTITY OF THE PREDATOR!
I MAY NOT HAVE GREEN LANTERN'S POWER ANYMORE, BUT I'M STILL A MAN WITHOUT FEAR, AND THAT BEATING HE GAVE ME MAKES ME THAT MUCH MORE DETERMINED TO GET HIM!

GOOD, HAL! YOU NEED SOMETHING TO SINK YOUR TEETH INTO! AND WE BOTH NEED TO KNOW WHY HE SEEMS TO--LOVE ME--!
THAT'S FOR SURE!

NOW HERE'S MY PLAN--!

HA HA HA HA HA HA
HA HA HA HA

BURBANK--
TAWNY, I WANT TO TALK TO YOU!
YES, MR. LINDERS?

TAWNY, I'M AN OLD NEWSMAN! I'M OUT OF STYLE! BUT I FEEL, AS YOUR BOSS, THAT YOU'RE PUTTING TOO MUCH OPINION INTO YOUR PIECES
TOO MUCH, PERHAPS--OF YOUR PERSONAL LIFE! YOU'VE INTERVIEWED STEWART TWICE ALREADY--!
PEOPLE ARE WATCHING, MR. LINDERS!

YEAH--I KNOW!
THE NETWORK CALLED! THEY WANT YOU FOR A WEST COAST CORRESPONDENT!
I TOLD YOU, I'M OUT OF STYLE--AND YOU'RE IN!

SOMEWHERE OVER THE IONO-SPHERE, ON THEIR WAY BACK FROM OA--
WELL, I HAD TO EXPECT IT, I GUESS--!
I NEVER EXPECTED TO BE THE G.L. WHEN I STARTED THAT STUFF, THOUGH!

WHY DO YOU WEAR A MASK NOW, JOHN?
I THOUGHT, AS THE G.L., I SHOULD WEAR THE OUTFIT, KATMA TUI!
HOW WAS I TO KNOW THE MASK WAS OP-TIONAL--THAT HALF YOU ALIEN G.L.'S LET YOUR BARE FACES HANG OUT?
JUST MORE IGNORANCE ON MY PART!

HOLLYWOOD--
YOUR PEOPLE DON'T SEEM TO SHARE YOUR LOW OPINION OF YOURSELF, JOHN!
--AND THERE IS NO NEED TO USE MY FULL NAME, ACTUALLY!
OKAY, KATMA! BUT MY LOW OPINION'S NOT OF MYSELF! IT'S OF THE WAY THE GUARDIANS TRAINED ME FOR THIS JOB!

MARINA DEL REY--
OR DIDN'T TRAIN ME!
A CALL EVERY YEAR OR SO, THEN BACK TO A LIFE IN ARCHITECTURE BE-TWEEN TIMES! THAT DOESN'T QUALIFY ME TO PATROL A SPACE SECTOR!
THEY UNDERSTAND THAT NOW! SO I WILL BE BESIDE YOU UNTIL EVERY-ONE AGREES THAT YOU ARE FULLY TRAINED!

THE MARINA CITY TOWERS--
DID THE FIRST GREEN LANTERN NEED A LOT OF TRAINING?
I DO NOT KNOW! HE JOINED THE CORPS BEFORE I DID!
SO YOU KNOW WHO HE IS?
YES--BUT IF THE GUARDIANS WOULD NOT TELL YOU, NEITHER WILL I!

BETTER THAT YOU DO NOT KNOW THAT HAL JORDAN WOULD PUSH ME TO ABANDON LOVE FOR THE SAKE OF THE CORPS--
--THEN ABANDON THE CORPS HIMSELF FOR THE SAKE OF HIS OWN LOVE.
BETTER THAT YOU THINK YOUR PREDECESSOR AN HONORABLE MAN!

WELL, MAKE YOURSELF AT HOME! IT'S JUST A SUBLET, FOR WHILE I'M ON THE COAST, BUT YOU CAN STAY HERE IF YOU WANT --THAT IS, IF YOU DON'T MIND MY HAVING LADIES OVER NOW AND AGAIN--

--AND, IF YOU DON'T MIND MY MAKING STUPID REMARKS LIKE THAT NOW AND AGAIN!
IT'S JUST--ALMOST TOO MUCH FOR ONE MAN TO HOLD TOGETHER, KATMA! GREEN LANTERN FOR A WEEK NOW--ALL THE THINGS I HAVE TO LEARN THERE--
--AND THEN ALL THE CHANGES IT'S GOING TO MAKE IN MY PERSONAL LIFE! I DON'T SUPPOSE THERE'LL BE ANY LADIES AROUND FOR SOME TIME NOW, OTHER THAN YOU!

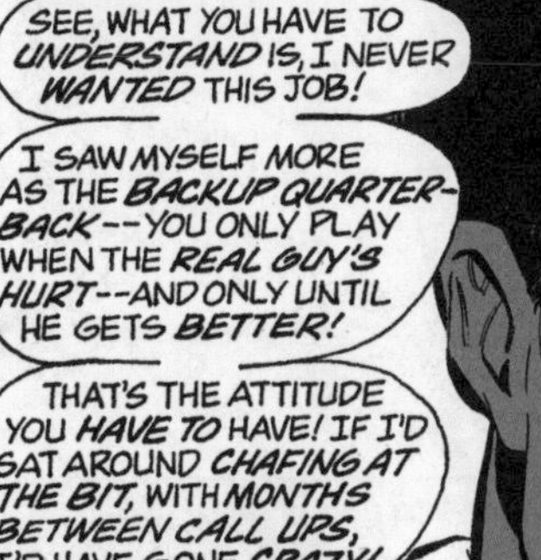

SEE, WHAT YOU HAVE TO UNDERSTAND IS, I NEVER WANTED THIS JOB!
I SAW MYSELF MORE AS THE BACKUP QUARTER-BACK--YOU ONLY PLAY WHEN THE REAL GUY'S HURT--AND ONLY UNTIL HE GETS BETTER!
THAT'S THE ATTITUDE YOU HAVE TO HAVE! IF I'D SAT AROUND CHAFING AT THE BIT, WITH MONTHS BETWEEN CALL UPS, I'D HAVE GONE CRAZY!
AND HEY--I LOVE ARCHITECTURE! THEY CALL ME "SQUARE" JOHN STEWART FOR A REASON!

BUT DON'T WORRY--I'M NOT ABOUT TO LET THE TEAM DOWN! IF I'M GOING TO PLAY, I'M GOING TO BE THE BEST THERE EVER WAS AT THIS GAME! BETTER EVEN THAN THE LAST GUY, WHOEVER HE WAS!
THAT'S WHY MY LACK OF TRAINING REALLY BUGS ME!

BUT WITH YOUR HELP, I--
WHA--

WOW!
I THOUGHT I WOULD DRAW STARES WITH CRIMSON SKIN, SO I USED MY RING TO MATCH YOUR COLOR, JOHN!
GUESS WHAT, LADY--YOU'RE STILL GONNA DRAW STARES--!

MOSTLY MINE--!
NOW, JOHN--

ENCINAL CANYON--
BLASH!

"BETTER THAN THE OLD GREEN LANTERN," EH? THAT REMAINS TO BE SEEN!
BUT HE IS BIG NEWS NOW AND THAT IS HIS MOST IMPORTANT FEATURE!
IT IS IMPERATIVE THAT I BE SEEN BY ALL-- THAT MY STORY MAKE WORLD-WIDE HEADLINES--

KRAKK!
--WHEN I, SONAR OF MODORA THE MASTER OF SOUND, DESTROY HIM UTTERLY!

AND FINALLY, IN THE QUIET COMMUNITY OF TORRANCE, THOMAS "PIEFACE" KALMAKU IS JUST ARRIVING HOME...

HE DOESN'T WATCH TV ANYMORE...

OVERNIGHT, THE NEWS ABOUT GREEN LANTERN SWEEPS ON ACROSS THE COUNTRY, AND BY THE FOLLOWING MORNING, MILLIONS MORE HAVE BEEN GALVANIZED--
--BUT FOR HAL JORDAN, ARRIVING FOR SOME PRIVATE WORK AT FERRIS AIRCRAFT, IT'S ALREADY FORGOTTEN!
SORT OF...

AFTER ALL, TODAY'S THE TENTH DAY OF THE REST OF HIS LIFE!
THE PREDATOR MUST BE ASSOCIATED WITH THE COMPANY SOMEHOW! HE KNOWS HIS WAY AROUND TOO WELL TO BE AN OUTSIDER!
AND IT'S MY GUESS THAT HE KILLED OUR ENEMY JASON BLOCH! BLOCH WAS CUT UP BADLY, AND MR.P HAS CLAWS ALL OVER HIM!
PERSONNEL

THEN THERE ARE HIS APPROACHES TO CAROL--!

SO LET'S HAVE A LOOK AT THE PERSONNEL RECORDS! PEOPLE WITH A FIXATION ON CAROL, OR HER COMPANY--

AH! THERE'S TOM!
HI! TOM!

STILL MAD AT ME FOR NOT CONSULTING HIM ABOUT MY QUITTING THE CORPS, I GUESS!
WELL, HE'LL GET OVER IT! I CAN'T BE EXPECTED TO THINK OF EVERYTHING--!

YEAH! HOORAH!!!
WHAT'S THAT--? CHEERING--?
DID WE GET A NEW CONTRACT--

OH!

JOHN, YOU SON OF A GUN!
CAN YOU BELIEVE IT? WE HAD GREEN LANTERN WORKING RIGHT HERE!
JOHN, WHY DIDN'T YOU TELL US?
HEY-- HEY--
--THANKS A LOT, EVERYBODY, BUT LET'S BE COOL NOW! I'M STILL THE SAME GUY, WHATEVER CLOTHES I HAVE ON--
--AND THESE CLOTHES ARE THE CLOTHES OF AN ARCHITECT -- AN ARCHITECT WHO'S GOT A JOB TO DO HERE, JUST LIKE YOU DO!
JOHN--

I'M SORRY, JOHN, BUT THAT'S NO LONGER TRUE!
I'M GOING TO HAVE TO LAY YOU OFF!

WHAT--?
MS. FERRIS, YOU CAN'T--!
YES, I CAN! MY MIND'S MADE UP. I DON'T WANT FERRIS AIRCRAFT ASSOCIATED WITH GREEN LANTERN ANYMORE, IN ANY WAY, SHAPE, OR FORM!
YOU'VE DONE A GREAT JOB, JUST AS HAL SAID YOU WOULD, BUT--
HAL? HAL JORDAN--?

WHY WOULD HE RECOMMEND ME? I DIDN'T KNOW HIM BEFORE--!
OH, WELL, NO-- I DIDN'T--
UH-OH! BETTER TALK FAST!
THERE'S NO MYSTERY, JOHN! YOU'VE GOT A SOLID REPUTATION! I READ ABOUT YOU SOMEPLACE--

HAL!!
HOW GOOD TO SEE YOU, YOU OLD DEVIL!
KATMA TUI! WHAT-- MMMFF!

WHAT WAS THAT ALL ABOUT??
HONEST, CAROL, I CAN EXPLAIN EVERYTHING-- I THINK! SHE'S REALLY ANOTHER GREEN LANTERN, UPSET WITH ME--AND YOU, SEE--
WHY, I WAS JUST GETTING BACK AT CAROL FERRIS--FOR YOU, JOHN! SHE ENDED YOUR JOB, SO I THOUGHT I WOULD TRY TO CONFOUND HER RELATIONSHIP WITH--
--THAT BOYFRIEND OF HERS!
THIS IS VERY CONFUSING! I MUST NOT ALLOW JOHN TO SUSPECT THAT HAL AND I KNOW EACH OTHER, OR HE WOULD GUESS WHO HAL WAS--
--BUT I COULD NOT BEAR TO SEE HAL AND CAROL TOGETHER!
I WONDER IF THE GUARDIANS MADE THE CORRECT CHOICE, SENDING ME HERE--!
WELL, YOU'RE SURE A BUNDLE OF SURPRISES, KAT! LET'S JUST GET OUT OF HERE BEFORE ANYTHING ELSE HAPPENS--
BA-LOOM!!

AH, MAN! I JUST GOT THIS BUILDING FIXED--!
COME FORTH AND FIGHT, GREEN LANTERN! COME FORTH AND FACE YOUR MASTER--
--SONAR, OF MODORA!

YOU GOT IT, JACK!

SONAR--?
I'VE NEVER HEARD OF HIM!
WELL, DON'T BLOW YOUR I.D.! STAY HERE, WHILE I SEE WHAT I CAN DO!

AND SO ONCE MORE, A SWATH OF GLORIOUS GREEN KNIFES THROUGH THE LOS ANGELES SKIES--

SONAR, HUH? SOUNDS TO ME LIKE SOME MASTER OF SOUND!

EXACTLY RIGHT, GREEN LANTERN!

YEA, JOHN!

PLOW

A MASTER WHO RIDES SOUND VIBRATIONS-- AND THROWS A SUPERSONIC PUNCH!

TWENTY FEET SEPARATED THEM, BUT THE SHOCK WAVE FILLED THAT SPACE JUST FINE!
HOLY--!
DO YOU SEE, PEOPLE? I, A PROUD CITIZEN OF MODORA, IN THE HEART OF EUROPE, HAVE BESTED YOUR AMERICAN HERO!
MODORA IS A TINY COUNTRY, OFTEN OVERLOOKED, BUT AS OF TODAY, IT OUTSHINES YOURS!

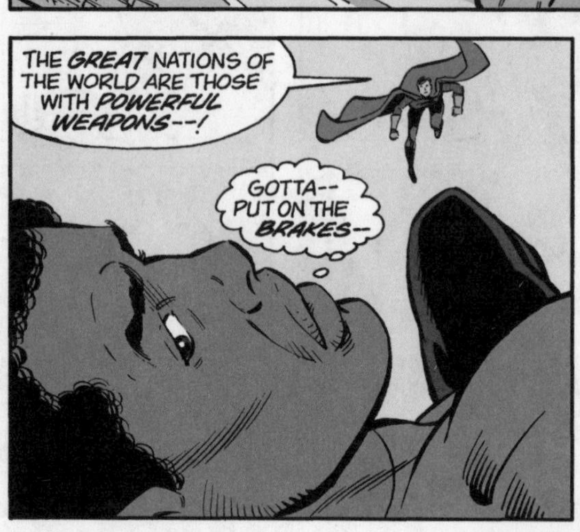
THE GREAT NATIONS OF THE WORLD ARE THOSE WITH POWERFUL WEAPONS--!
GOTTA-- PUT ON THE BRAKES--

WMP!

SUPRISED ME-- BUT--I BETTER GET USED TO BEING SURPRISED
THAT'S NO EXCUSE ANYMORE--!
HEY, SONAR--

--I CAN BREAK THE SOUND BARRIER, TOO!

GOOD, LANTERN! GOOD! YOUR PREDECESSOR NEVER THOUGHT OF THAT!
KRRIP!
STILL, THERE ARE OTHER THINGS TO BE DONE WITH SOUND--!

HURLING THOSE GIRDERS ON THE CRESTS OF HIS SOUND WAVES--!

I'LL LET HIM SCORE ON SOMETHING ELSE!
DAMMIT, HE'S TEARING UP ALL MY WORK!
SPONG!!

BELOW, THE CROWD SURGES FORWARD, SPELLBOUND-- ALL THE CROWD!
LOOK OUT! YOU DON'T KNOW WHAT HIS SONIC GUN CAN DO!
GET IN CLOSE BEFORE HE CAN USE IT AGAIN--

NO! IT'S HIS FIGHT NOW!
I'M OUT OF IT!

CAREFUL, LANTERN-- TURBULENT AIR!
S-S-SOUND W-WAVES! I-IT'S A-A-ALL--

K-KAT--!

I HEAR YOU, JOHN! I'LL BE RIGHT THERE!
N-NO! ALL I NEED'S-- YOUR POWER!
SOUND WAVES! THEY'RE EITHER IN PHASE, OR THEY'RE NOT!
STAY UNDER COVER--BUT DO WHAT I DO!

INSTANTLY, THE EMERALD GLADIATOR LOOSES A WALL OF PULSATING POWER AT THE MODORAN!

FOOL! I CAN ABSORB ALL THAT ENERGY, AND RETURN IT!

BUT THE NEXT MOMENT--

EH? MORE SOUND WAVES, FROM BEHIND ME! BUT I CAN ABSORB EVEN THAT!

NOT IF I SKIP JUST HALF A BEAT, SUCKER!

ONE MOMENT THE SKY IS FILLED WITH SOUND--

--THE NEXT, ALL IS DEAD SILENCE!
TWO WAVE FRONTS--CANCELING EACH OTHER OUT--!

NOTHING LEFT--
--TO DRAW ON--
--ANY--

--M--
UMP!

YOU DID IT, JOHN! YOU DID IT!
YEAH! I SURE DID, DIDN'T I?

TAWNY YOUNG, GALAXY BROADCASTING, JOHN. THIS TIME WE ARRIVED IN TIME TO GET EVERYTHING ON TAPE!
THAT ECHO TRICK--HOW DID YOU DO THAT?
TAWNY--WHEN I'M DRESSED LIKE THIS--IT'S NOT "JOHN"--

--IT'S "GREEN LANTERN"!

WELL, THAT'S THAT...
NOW, AS TO THE PREDATOR...
PERSONNEL

DEEP WITHIN THE PLANET CALLED **OA**, THERE IS A PLACE CALLED **THE HALL OF GREAT SERVICE**.
DEEP WITHIN THE HALL OF GREAT SERVICE, THERE IS A TOME CALLED **THE BOOK OF WORTHY NAMES**...


...AND DEEP WITHIN THE BOOK OF WORTHY NAMES IS A YOUNG AND IMPRESSIONABLE MEMBER OF THE GREEN LANTERN CORPS.

*HER NAME IS ARISIA.*

**TOMAR RE**, THIS IS ABSOLUTELY **WILD**! I'D NEVER **REALIZED** BEFORE JUST HOW **MANY** GREEN LANTERNS THERE **WERE**.

ALL THESE **NAMES**... FAMOUS ONES LIKE **HAL JORDAN** AND **KATMA TUI**, INFAMOUS ONES LIKE **SINESTRO**...

...AND SO MANY THAT I'VE NEVER EVEN **HEARD** OF! WHO THE HOBLAT IS **LEEZLE PON**? OR **DKRTZY RRR**? OR **MOGO**?

I'VE NEVER MET THESE PEOPLE. DON'T THEY ATTEND **MEETINGS**?

THERE ARE SOME GREEN LANTERNS WHO **CANNOT** ATTEND MEETINGS. **LEEZLE PON**, FOR EXAMPLE, IS A **SUPERINTELLIGENT SMALLPOX VIRUS**.
**DKRTZY RRR**, ON THE OTHER HAND, **DOES** ATTEND MEETINGS. BUT SINCE HE IS AN **ABSTRACT MATHEMATICAL PROGRESSION**, ONLY THE **GUARDIANS** NOTICE HIS PRESENCE.

AND AS FOR **MOGO**...
WELL, MOGO DOESN'T **SOCIALIZE**.

THERE IS A STORY ABOUT MOGO THAT YOU MAY FIND INTERESTING.
IT BEGINS WITH A CREATURE KNOWN AS BOLPHUNGA THE UNRELENTING...
TALES OF THE GREEN LANTERN CORPS
MOGO DOESN'T SOCIALIZE
ALAN MOORE: WRITER / DAVE GIBBONS: ARTIST-LETTERER / ANTHONY TOLLIN: colorist / LEN WEIN: EDITOR.
"BOLPHUNGA POSSESSED THE STRENGTH OF A DENEBIAN DOZER-BULL, THE ENDURANCE OF A LALOTIAN LAVA-LIMPET...
"...AND THE INTELLIGENCE OF A BED OF KELP.
"HIS REPUTATION WAS BUILT UPON NUMEROUS SUCCESSFUL DUELS, AND A STRING OF VANQUISHED FOES RENT LIMB FROM LIMB...
"HE'D PULVERIZED RUSTANG THE VINDICTIVE. HE'D PUREED THE TERRIFYING KLOBA VUD. HE'D BROKEN SEVENTEEN OF RIVERA'S ARMS.
"NOW HE INTENDED TO CAP HIS DUBIOUS CAREER BY CHALLENGING THE MOST FEARED AND MYSTERIOUS BEING OF THEM ALL...
"...THE GREEN LANTERN KNOWN AS MOGO."
2

MOGO, YOU SKULKING COWARD--I KNOW NOT WHERE UPON THIS OVER-GROWN PLANET YOU ARE, BUT HEAR THIS...
I AM BOLPHUNGA THE UNRELENTING, AND I COME TO CLEAVE YOU FROM WEEZAND TO FORK!
AYE, YOU HEARD ARIGHT, POOR DOOMED AND COWERING ONE!
BOLPHUNGA AT WHOSE NAM THE DESERTS TREMBLE AND THE MOUNTAINS BURST INTO TEARS. BOLPHUNGA, SON OF BOFF!
I OFFER YOU A CHOICE, MEWLING AND RELUCTANT CUR...
DELIVER YOURSELF UNTO MY MERCIES NOW, AND I WILL PERMIT YOU TO LIVE, ALBEIT ONLY IN A LIFE-SUPPORT SYSTEM!
CONTINUE TO AVOID MY AWESOME GAZE, AND YOU WILL FIND ME LESS GENEROUS!
WHICH IS IT TO BE?
VERY WELL! YOUR CRAVEN SILENCE SPEAKS LOUDLY OF YOUR BASE INTENT!
PREPARE YOURSELF, O SICKLY AND TREMULOUS ADVERSARY...
...PREPARE YOURSELF FOR THE COMING OF BOLPHUNGA!!
3

"AND SO, OFF LUMBERED BOLPHUNGA INTO THE DENSE GREEN JUNGLES OF THE WORLD ON WHICH HE'D BEEN TOLD MOGO WAS TO BE FOUND...

"THE SEARCH WAS NOT AN EASY ONE. FOR ONE THING, BOLPHUNGA HAD BEEN ABLE TO GLEAN NO INFORMATION AS TO WHAT MOGO ACTUALLY LOOKED LIKE.
"COULD HE BE A PLANT...?

"...OR PERHAPS AN INSECT?"
NO...
NO POWER RING ON THIS ONE...

"INDEED, TRY AS HE MIGHT, BOLPHUNGA COULD FIND NO TRACE OF INTELLIGENT LIFE UPON THE PLANET AT ALL...
"...SAVE FOR ONE THING.

"THE FOLIAGE HAD OBVIOUSLY BEEN CUT AND TENDED BY SOME HIGHER LIFE-FORM.

"THERE WERE NEAT-EDGED CLEARINGS, KILOMETERS WIDE. THERE WERE PLACES WHERE THE GREENERY HAD BEEN CLIPPED INTO VAST AND INDECIPHERABLE SHAPES.

"AS WEEKS TURNED INTO MONTHS AND MONTHS EXTENDED INTO YEARS, BOLPHUNGA GREW METHODICAL IN HIS SEARCH, DRAWING MANY PAINSTAKING MAPS...

"NOT FOR NOTHING WAS HE CALLED 'THE UNRELENTING.'

4

"...BUT STILL THERE WAS NO TRACE OF MOGO. AND THEN, ONE EVENING..."
HE HAS TO BE HERE SOMEWHERE! LET ME CONSULT MY MAPS ONCE MORE...
PAH! THEY GIVE ME NO CLUE AT ALL!
NOTHING SAVE FOR THESE MEANING-LESS SWATHS CUT INTO THE...
...GREENERY?
YAAAAGH!
"AND IT WAS THEN THAT BOLPHUNGA THE UNRELENTING FINALLY ...WELL, RELENTED, I SUPPOSE."
AAAAAAAAAA
AAAAAAAAAAAAAAAAAAA
"CLAMBERING HURRIEDLY INTO HIS COSMOCRUISER, HE CAREENED OFF INTO THE VOID, A PITIFUL BLOB OF WAILING TERROR.
5

"AS HIS CRAFT BURST FREE OF THE UPPER ATMOSPHERE, HE LOOKED BACK ONCE...
"LOOKED BACK AT THE CARPET OF FOREST THAT COVERED A CONTINENT, LOOKED BACK AT THE DESIGN CARVED INTO THAT FOREST...
"LOOKED BACK...
"AND SAW THE GREEN LANTERN KNOWN AS MOGO..."
...AND THAT, ARISIA, IS WHY MOGO DOESN'T SOCIALIZE.
IT'S HIS GRAVITY FIELD, YOU SEE. IT WOULD PULL OA APART.
OF COURSE, ONE DAY I'LL HAVE TO TELL YOU ABOUT SOME OF THE REALLY BIG GREEN LANTERNS...
TOMAR RE? YOU'RE JOKING, RIGHT? THAT WAS ALL JUST A WAD OF SKUBITZNY, WASN'T IT?
WASN'T IT?
TOMAR RE?
6
THE END.

# CHANGING THE GUARD

**Writer:** RON MARZ **Penciller:** DARRYL BANKS **Inker:** ROMEO TANGHAL

Originally presented in GREEN LANTERN No. 51, May 1994

In 1994, GREEN LANTERN was struggling. With the success of the "Death of Superman" storyline and subsequent "Knightfall" storyline that saw Batman replaced, major changes were being made across the DC Universe. The most controversial, and seemingly permanent, was Hal Jordan's fall from grace. In "Emerald Twilight," Hal lost Coast City, went mad with power and left his fellow Green Lanterns for dead in the depths of space.

The only remaining Guardian at the time, Ganthet, went to Earth and gave the ring to a young artist walking through an alley – Kyle Rayner. Like Guy Gardner and John Stewart, Kyle Rayner became an icon in his own right. Created by Ron Marz and Darryl Banks, Kyle brought a whole new perspective to the idea of being a Green Lantern. Gone were the Corps and the Guardians. Kyle was the only one in the universe with a power ring.

I chose this story for several reasons, the first being a symbol of the contributions by Ron and Darryl. With their explosive storyline and the introduction of Kyle, they brought readers back to GREEN LANTERN. For years, although a solid book, GREEN LANTERN had not set the universe on fire. They pushed the envelope as far as it would go by making the lead hero into the lead villain, but it was interesting.

I've made mention that Kyle Rayner was the torchbearer, the one who kept the green light burning when the Corps had died out. In a way, I equate that with Ron. I meant that for Ron. He had the task of introducing a brand new character to wear the power ring while at the same time vilifying Jordan. It was no easy task. The story would undoubtedly upset longtime readers and wasn't guaranteed to bring in new ones, but he did it. And the popularity of Kyle even today is a testament to his work, and that of Grant Morrison and Howard Porter's run on JLA.

The second reason I chose this story is that it's good. It's fun to see someone attempting to learn about the ring for the first time. It'd been years, maybe longer, since the readers had seen a real rookie try on a power ring for size.

It would've been nice to see how Kyle would've reacted to Kilowog.

– Geoff Johns

MY NAME'S KYLE RAYNER.
AND I DON'T KNOW WHAT I'M DOING.
OR MAYBE YOU CAN TELL THAT.
SPECIAL ITEM
Silky Doll
Franklyn's of Hollywood
-NYLON
-LYCRA
SPHAASH

CHANGING THE GUARD
UNFORTUNATELY, I'M DISCOVERING A LITTLE INEXPERIENCE CAN GET A GUY KILLED.
CHANAL
BANKSTER
O BABY
YEAH, YEAH.
DON'T GET YOUR ELECTRODES IN AN UPROAR.

COME TO ME, BOY! FACE ME!
I'LL BURN YOU DOWN WITH THE POWER OF THE CITY ITSELF!
THIS WACKO'S CALLING HIMSELF OHM. LIKE THE ELECTRICAL UNIT.
GUESS I SHOULDN'T LAUGH. I'M CALLING MYSELF
GREEN LANTERN
RON MARZ WRITER
DARRYL BANKS PENCILS
ROMEO TANGHAL INKS
STEVE MATTSSON COLOR
ALBERT DE GUZMAN LETTERS
EDDIE BERGANZA ASSISTS
KEVIN DOOLEY Editor

I'M COMING FOR YOU!
LIKE I SAID, I'M PRETTY NEW TO ALL THIS.
WHICH IS NO REASON TO STOP ME FROM HURLING MYSELF AT A GUY IN A SEVEN-FOOT, HALF-TON SUIT OF ARMOR.
PROBABLY SHOULD BE, THOUGH.
SHRZAK
AARRR!

"...JUST LAST NIGHT."
NOK NOK NOK
C'MON, ALEX! OPEN UP!
WOULD YOU SHUT UP? YOU'LL WAKE MRS. KRAVITZ UPSTAIRS, AND YOU KNOW WHAT SHE'S LIKE.
GOD, KYLE, IT'S THE MIDDLE OF THE NIGHT. WHY SHOULD I LET YOU IN?
CAUSE YOU CAN'T RESIST ME.
OH?
THAT WHY WE BROKE UP LAST WEEK? OR WAS IT YOUR IRRESPONSIBILITY? OR ME TIRED OF DOING ALL THE WORK?
ANY OF THIS SOUNDING FAMILIAR?
YEAH, BUT SOMETHING'S HAPPENED.
UH HUH.

SO...
...WHAT'S THE BIG--

IS THIS COOL OR WHAT?

OH, YOU HAVE GOT TO BE KIDDING ME.

THIS IS THE DUMBEST STUNT YOU'VE EVER PULLED, KYLE.
HEY, HEY, THIS IS FOR REAL. I'M NOT FOOLING AROUND.
I MEAN, YEAH, IT'S HARD TO BELIEVE AND ALL, BUT...
...IT HAPPENED.

I'M IN THE ALLEY BEHIND THE HERETIC CLUB, RIGHT, TO GET SOME AIR...
...AND THIS BLUE MIDGET IN A RED DRESS JUST...APPEARS, YOU KNOW?
BLUE MIDGET IN A RED DRESS.
RIGHT. HE GIVES ME THIS RING, TELLS ME TO PUT IT ON, THEN DISAPPEARS. SO I DO...
...AND THIS HAPPENS. INSTANT SUIT.
MAN. I DON'T HAVE A CLUE WHAT'S GOING ON, BUT I HAD TO TELL SOMEBODY.
LUCKY ME.
YOU'RE REALLY NOT AKING THE CONNECTION ITH GREEN LANTERN?
WITH A WHAT?
NOT WHAT. WHO. GREEN LANTERN--THE HERO. THAT'S HIS COSTUME YOU'RE WEARING.
I GOT PIX OF HIM LAST MONTH WHEN THE PAPER SENT ME TO SHOOT THE AFTERMATH OF THE COAST CITY DISASTER.
YOUR SUIT IS THE SAME AS HIS. HE HAD A RING, TOO.
OH YEAH, THAT GUY. HE'S COOL. HE CAN DO STUFF WITH THE RING. FLY AND...
GEEZ, YOU THINK--
YES.!!!
ALL I HAVE TO DO IS THINK ABOUT IT, AND IT HAPPENS!
KYLE!

WHAT NEEDS TO HAPPEN IS FOR YOU TO GET YOUR FEET BACK ON THE GROUND.
THIS WHOLE THING IS... NUTS.
OKAY, SO LET'S SAY YOU'VE GOT SOMETHING HERE. WHAT DO YOU PLAN ON DOING WITH IT?
COME ON, ALEX. ISN'T IT OBVIOUS?
I'M GONNA BE A HERO.
A HERO? YOU CAN'T EVEN HOLD DOWN A JOB.
FREE-LANCE ARTIST IS A JOB.
BARELY ENOUGH OF ONE TO PAY YOUR RENT.
LOOK, MAYBE I DON'T UNDERSTAND EVERYTHING, BUT I DO KNOW THIS IS THE BIGGEST THING THAT'S EVER HAPPENED TO EITHER OF US.
WE'VE GOT A CHANCE TO DO SOMETHING WITH OUR LIVES.
YOU DON'T WANT TO BE SNAPPING GRIP-AND-GRINS FOR A RAG LIKE THE L.A. EXAMINER FOR THE REST OF YOUR LIFE...
...AND I DON'T WANT TO BE DESIGNING GREETING CARDS FOR THE REST OF MY MINE.

THIS ISN'T A RING, IT'S OUR TICKET OUT OF HERE. WE CAN GO SOMEWHERE AND BE SOMETHING.
I'M NOT EXACTLY CLOSE TO MY FAMILY, NEITHER ARE YOU. THERE'S NOTHING TO KEEP US HERE.
WE'LL GO TO NEW YORK, LIKE YOU'VE WANTED. I'LL DO THE HERO THING. YOU TAKE PICTURES OF ME.

WE CAN'T MISS. I'LL BE A MEDIA DARLING...
...AND THE NEW YORK TIMES'LL BE BEGGING YOU TO COME ON STAFF.

IT CAN WORK, ALEX. ALL OF IT... NEW YORK... ME AND YOU.
COME ON. HOW 'BOUT IT?
I DON'T... IT'S...
...IT'S JUST THAT...
...WELL...
...WELL ALL RIGHT.
ALL RIGHT!
YOU WON'T BE SORRY, ALEX, I PROMISE. FROM NOW ON, I'M THE MOST RESPONSIBLE GUY YOU KNOW.
YOU'D BETTER BE.
SO, UH, SINCE WE'RE BACK TOGETHER AND ALL, AND IT IS PRETTY LATE...
YOU DON'T KNOW WHEN TO STOP, DO YOU?
OKAY, OKAY, YOU CAN STAY.
COOL. I'LL JUST--
YOU'LL JUST HAUL YOUR BUTT OVER TO THE COUCH, ROMEO.
I HAVEN'T FORGIVEN YOU THAT MUCH YET.
I'LL SEE YOU...

"...IN THE MORNING."
RISE AND SHINE, SLEEPING BEAUTY. WE'VE GOT PLACES TO GO.
WHUUH!?
WH-WHAT'S GOIN' ON?
CALL CAME IN--SOME NUT IN A SUIT OF ARMOR IS TEARING UP RODEO DRIVE.
PAPER WANTS PICTURES, I COULD USE SOME COMPANY...
...AND I DON'T THINK I SHOULD LET YOU OUTTA MY SIGHT.
S-NODA
X-2000
WISH MY REGULAR CLOTHES WENT ON AS EASY AS THE COSTUME.
HANG ON A SEC. LET ME GET DRESSED...

"...AND WE'RE GONE."
WHAT, ARE WE TAKING THE SCENIC ROUTE HERE?
I'M TRYING TO MISS THE POLICE CORDONS. THE CLOSER I GET, THE BETTER MY SHOTS'LL BE.
COULD BE GOOD STUFF. APPARENTLY THIS GUY STOLE THE ARMOR FROM S.T.A.R. LABS, SOME KIND OF EXPERIMENTAL ELECTRICAL SUIT.
NOW HE'S TRYING TO PLUG INTO THE CITY'S ELECTRICAL SYSTEM AND SIPHON IT OFF TO POWER HIMS--
GEEZ.
LOOK AT THAT.

MORE POWER! GIVE ME MORE!
I'LL BRING THIS CITY TO ITS KNEES!
STAY PUT. I'M GOING TO GET CLOSE ENOUGH TO SHOOT A ROLL, THEN WE'LL GET THE HELL OUT OF HERE.
SURE YOU DON'T WANT--?
NO.
I MEAN IT, KYLE. JUST SIT TIGHT. DON'T DO ANYTHING STUPID...
...LIKE YOU USUALLY DO.
WHO, ME? I'M MR. RESPONSIBLE NOW, REMEMBER?
NO NEED TO WORRY ABOUT ME.
YOU GO DO YOUR THING. I'LL JUST SIT HERE AND WATCH.
Jeep

NOPE, I'M NOT GOING ANYWHERE. I'LL JUST SIT HERE...
...AND...
...WATCH.
Hmmm.
AH, THE HELL WITH IT.
LOOK OUT, WORLD! HERE COMES GREEN LANTERN
OH GREAT.

HEY.
YOU.
YOU'RE DONE, HEADCASE. GAME OVER.
AND YOU'RE GOING TO BE THE ONE TO STOP ME? YOU? I DON'T QUITE SEE HOW, BOY.
WELL, YOU SEE THIS RING, DON'T YOU?
SO?
SO?
SO... UM... SO THIS RING IS MORE THAN YOU CAN HANDLE. BELIEVE ME.
REALLY.

YOU'RE WASTING MY TIME.
HEY, DIDN'T YOU HEAR WHAT I--

ALL OF WHICH BRINGS US BACK TO THE HERE AND NOW.
UNFORTUNATELY.
SKRAAK
MAYBE I AM IN OVER MY HEAD. NOT THAT I'D EVER ADMIT IT, OF COURSE. ESPECIALLY TO ALEX.
I'D RATHER HAVE THIS GUY FRY ME THAN LISTEN TO "I TOLD YOU SO." SHE'S JUST SO GOOD AT TELLING ME THAT.
WELL...SHE HAS HAD A LOT OF PRACTICE.
FOR GOD'S SAKE! PROTECT YOURSELF.
SHE'S RIGHT.
CHOOOM
I CAN'T KEEP DODGING FOREVER. I NEED TO THINK ABOUT EVERYTHING THIS RING CAN DO.
I NEED TO CONCENTRATE.
HUNNF

IT'S JUST A MATTER OF WILLPOWER.
I CAN DO THIS!
A SHIELD!? A SHIELD'S NOT GOING TO SAVE YOU OR L.A.!
DAMN. HIS SHIELD'S BREAKING UP.
I KNOW THAT LOOK, KYLE. DON'T GET COCKY.
AAAGH!
OKAY, SO MAYBE I COULD USE A LITTLE PRACTICE.
I'M PLUGGED IN TO THE ENTIRE CITY! YOU CAN'T--
KRUNK
BUT THERE'S NO WAY I'M LETTING THIS JERK END MY CAREER 15 MINUTES INTO IT.
HGGN!

WHEN I'M DONE YOU'RE GONNA GET PLUGGED IN TO A NICE JAIL CELL.
AAH! DON'T! DON'T CUT ME!
SHUT UP. I KNOW WHAT I'M DOING.
HE'D BETTER HOPE I DO...
...ALTHOUGH A LACK OF CONFIDENCE WAS NEVER REALLY ONE OF MY SHORTCOMINGS.
CAN'T RECALL BEING AT A LOSS FOR WORDS TOO OFTEN EITHER.
COME ON OUTTA THERE, PRINCE ALBERT.
MAYBE THIS IS THE RIGHT LINE OF WORK FOR ME AFTER ALL.
NNG

YOU DID IT!
... HOLD STILL SO I CAN GET A PICTURE...
...ARE YOU ALL RIGHT?
MAN, ALEX IS THE BEST. WORRIED ABOUT ME AND STILL SNAPPING PICTURES.
SHE'S GOT THE EYE ALL RIGHT. MORE TALENT THAN I'LL EVER HAVE.
ALL RIGHT? I'M GREAT!
I KICKED HIS BUTT! DID YOU SEE...
GREEN LANTERN!
HEY!
GREEN LANTERN!
ONE DAY PEOPLE ARE GOING TO TALK ABOUT ALEXANDRA DeWITT IN THE SAME BREATH AS CARTIER-BRESSON, SALGADO, MARY ELLEN MARK.

AND TALK ABOUT ME IN THE SAME BREATH AS SUPERMAN AND BATMAN.
WHO... ME?
YOU WERE WONDERFUL!
I REMEMBER YOU! YOU SAVED ME ABOUT FIVE YEARS AGO?
HIS HAIR LOOK DIFFERENT TO YOU?
WELL... UH...

THANK YOU. THANK YOU. I WAS MERELY DOING MY HEROIC DUTY.
AS ANY ONE OF YOU MIGHT--

OKAY, HERO, THAT'S ENOUGH.
WE'D BETTER GET YOU...

"...SOMEPLACE A LITTLE LESS CROWDED."

YOU REALLY THINK SO?

YEAH, I MEAN, IT JUST SEEMS LIKE THE *RIGHT* THING TO DO.

I DON'T KNOW. I KINDA LIKE THE *OLD ONE*.

IT LOOKS *GOOD* ON ME.

TRUE...

...BUT THAT'S NOT REALLY *YOUR* COSTUME, IS IT? IT BELONGS TO *SOMEBODY ELSE*.

YOU NEED *YOUR OWN* IDENTITY.

GUESS THAT MAKES *SENSE*. AND *I AM* A GRAPHIC DESIGNER.

SO GO FOR IT.
WHAT, YOU MEAN NOW?
YEAH, WHY NOT? THERE'S NOBODY AROUND.
RAIDERS
LET ME THINK ABOUT THIS...

SO?
WHATCHA THINK?
WELL, IT'S GOT DEFINITE POSSIBILITIES, KIDDO. WE'LL JUST HAVE TO WAIT AND SEE WHAT HAPPENS, WON'T WE?
RAIDERS
RAIDERS

# TYGERS

**Writer:** ALAN MOORE **Artist:** KEVIN O'NEILL

Originally presented in GREEN LANTERN CORPS ANNUAL No. 2, 1986

The last story in this collection is perhaps the most likely to be included and maybe the most unlikely.

Although he only wrote a handful of stories, Alan Moore made an impression. One of those stories, "Tygers," illustrated by Kevin O'Neill, redefined Hal Jordan's predecessor, Abin Sur.

Abin Sur had crashed on Earth in a spacecraft. But it was clear the power ring allowed its user to fly through space. The ring created a protective aura. So why?

Alan Moore deftly made it about character. About fear. Yellow was never a Lantern's main weakness. It was fear. It always should be fear. Something that reaches to the heart of a character rather than a piece of a plot. Within "Tygers" you'll see what Abin's great fear and failure was as the Empire of Tears attempts to break him.

This story also introduced a prophecy that the enemies of the Corps would one day unite and take down even the strongest Lantern of them all, the Daxamite Sodam Yat.

The idea of a "Revelations" for the Green Lantern Corps was captivating. Dave introduced Sodam Yat into the GREEN LANTERN CORPS. While I was gearing up for my own work on Green Lantern I thought hard. If there really was a "Revelations" for the Green Lantern Corps, what would it actually be What would it be called?

I thought about it. For a long time.

Then finally I knew. There could be no other nam for it than "The Blackest Night."

"The Blackest Night" was a piece of the Oath th was spoken, but never quite literal. Well, what if was? What if the skies would go black and all lig would be extinguished? Would that not be the ultima end of a police force that shined their light for justice

It is the wonderful mythology of the Green Lante Corps that allows our imaginations to go to the farthe reaches of space, emotion and what it is to be aliv What are the true struggles of life? Are they simp "bad guys" we can punch our way through? Or is more than that? Is it a yellow sign or is it the fear we' held onto since we were children? Is it the rage in o hearts for the tragedies we've had to face? Or is it invading army of bloodthirsty aliens? Is it the hope th we must grab onto to carry on in those dark days or it an enemy forever wanting to take away what y have? Is it within our own souls or outside our contr

Or is it both? Is it all of these and more?

It is in a universe patrolled by Hal Jordan and t Green Lantern Corps.

– Geoff Joh

PROLOGUE:

YEARS LATER, HE DIED.
COLLIDING WITH THE RADIATION GIRDLE OF THE TURQUOISE PLANET, HIS SHIP SUFFERED A CRITICAL MALFUNCTION.
HIS RING OF POWER WAS SIMILARLY USELESS. THERE WAS NOTHING HE COULD DO.

HE WATCHED HELPLESSLY AS THE MELANOMA DRIVE BEGAN TO DEVOUR ITSELF, AND HE KNEW THEN THAT HE HAD BEEN DECEIVED.
HAD HE RELIED UPON THE RING ALONE, PERHAPS HE NEED NOT HAVE PERISHED.
HE FELL...

...AND ALL THE WAY DOWN, IN HIS MIND, HE COULD HEAR THEM LAUGHING.

TALES OF THE GREEN LANTERN CORPS

# TALES

ALAN MOORE writer
KEVIN O'NEILL Artist
JOHN COSTANZA letterer
ANTHONY TOLLIN colorist
WEIN/HELFER editor

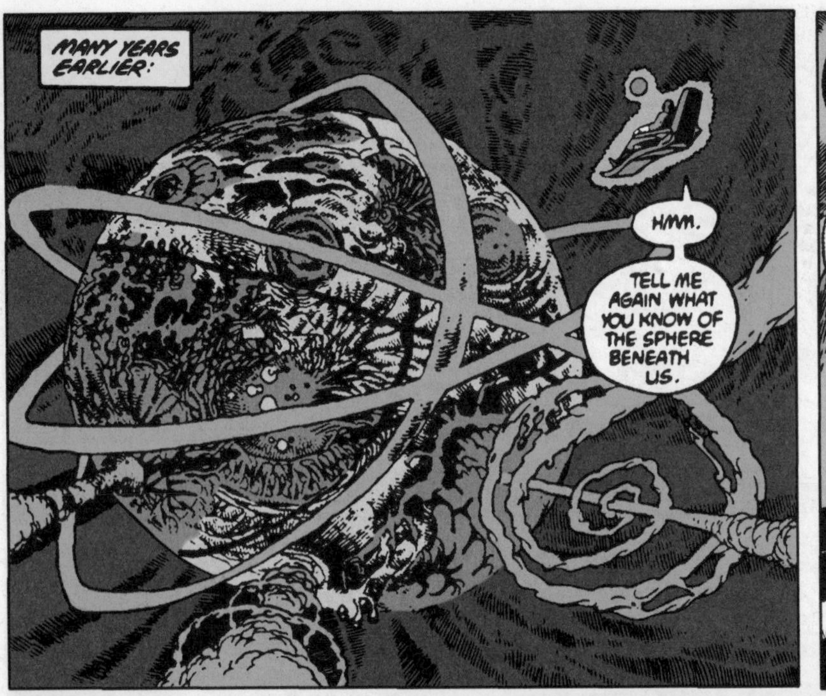
MANY YEARS EARLIER:
HMM.
TELL ME AGAIN WHAT YOU KNOW OF THE SPHERE BENEATH US.

THE ORB IS NAMED YSMAULT, ABIN SUR. A LIFELESS WORLD DEIGNED FORBIDDEN TERRITORY BY THE GUARDIANS OF OA, WHOM YOU SERVE.
MANY MILLENNIA AGO, IT WAS THE THRONEWORLD OF THE DISMAL EMPIRE OF TEARS.

"DURING THE NIGHT-EONS WHEN MAGIC HELD PROMINENCE, THE EMPIRE OF TEARS SPANNED THREE GALAXIES.
"ITS REGENTS, DEATHLESS AND MALIGN ESSENCES WHOSE CRUELTIES HAD GROWN TOO SOPHISTICATED FOR MORTAL FORM, REIGNED UNCHALLENGED...

"...UNTIL THE ELDERS OF OA DECLARED THEMSELVES GUARDIANS OF THE UNIVERSE, COMMENCING WITH A PURGE OF DARK AND NECROMANTIC FACTIONS FROM THE STARWAYS.
"THE EMPIRE OF TEARS WAS NO MORE. THE DEMONS WERE CHAINED..."

...BUT NOT DEAD. THOUGH DISEMBODIED AND PHYSICALLY POWERLESS, THEIR SUBTLE AND DANGEROUS MINDS REMAIN ENTOMBED UPON YSMAULT.
IT IS A CORPSE-WORLD, HAUNTED BY ITS DEAD MASTERS, AND NONE MAY GO THERE SAVE BY THE GUARDIANS' LEAVE.
2

THE GUARDIANS ARE PARSECS HENCE, TOO FAR AWAY TO ASK PERMISSION. IS THIS TRULY THE WORLD UPON WHICH THE CRIPPLED SHIP THAT I DETECTED HAS CRASHED?
IT IS.
THEN I HAVE NO CHOICE...
...OTHER THAN DESCENT INTO THE MAELSTROM.

BY THAT FIRST AND FINAL HAND...

...WHAT IS IT, THAT CREATES SUCH AN ATMOSPHERE?
NITROGEN (61.39 PERCENT); OXYGEN (16.04 PERCENT); NEON (12.26 PERCENT); METHANE (9.57 PERCENT);...

I DO NOT SPEAK OF THIS WORLD'S MANTLE OF GASES...
... BUT RATHER OF ITS BITTER AND POISONOUS LANDSCAPE, ITS SILENCE MADE OF SUGGESTIVE WHISPERS TOO SOFT TO HEAR.
3

A GREEN LANTERN? AFTER SO LONG?
ABIN SUR! HE'S CALLED ABIN SUR...
A GREEN LANTERN! HERE! JUST THINK...

SHOW YOURSELVES!

WE STAND UNCONCEALED, ABIN SUR...
...AS WE HAVE STOOD SINCE YOUR OAN MASTERS ENTOMBED US IN THESE FORMS, AGES AGO.
...BUT DO NOT SUPPOSE WE BEAR A GRUDGE, ABIN SUR. WE WISH ONLY TO HELP...

WHY, THAT'S RIGHT, ABIN SUR, YOU HAVE ONLY TO ASK...
IS THERE SOME WOMAN YOU DESIRE? OR PERHAPS THE POWER TO OVERTHROW YOUR BLUE-SKINNED MASTERS, WHO DESPISE YOU AND UNDER-VALUE YOUR ABILITIES?

BEGONE, ILLUSIONS.
YOU HAVE NOTHING THAT I DESIRE.

HAVEN'T WE?
HAVEN'T WE?
HAVEN'T WE?
HAVEN'T WE?
HAVEN'T WE?
4

AND WHO WOULD YOU BE FLATTERER?
I DO NOT FLATTER. I MERELY SPEAK THAT WHICH IS TRUE.
I AM QULL OF THE FIVE INVERSIONS.

A LEAGUE TO THE WEST. THERE IS ONE SURVIVOR... A CHILD...
WHAT ARE YOUR OTHER TWO QUESTIONS?

I THINK THAT WILL WAIT...
...AT LEAST UNTIL I HAVE EVALUATED THE VERACITY OF YOUR FIRST ANSWER.

THE CHILD HAS A BROKEN ANKLE, BUT IS OTHERWISE UN-HARMED BY HER PASSAGE THROUGH OUR WORLD...
WHEREAS YOU, ABIN SUR...

...YOU STILL HAVE TWO MORE QUESTIONS.

WELL, ABIN SUR?

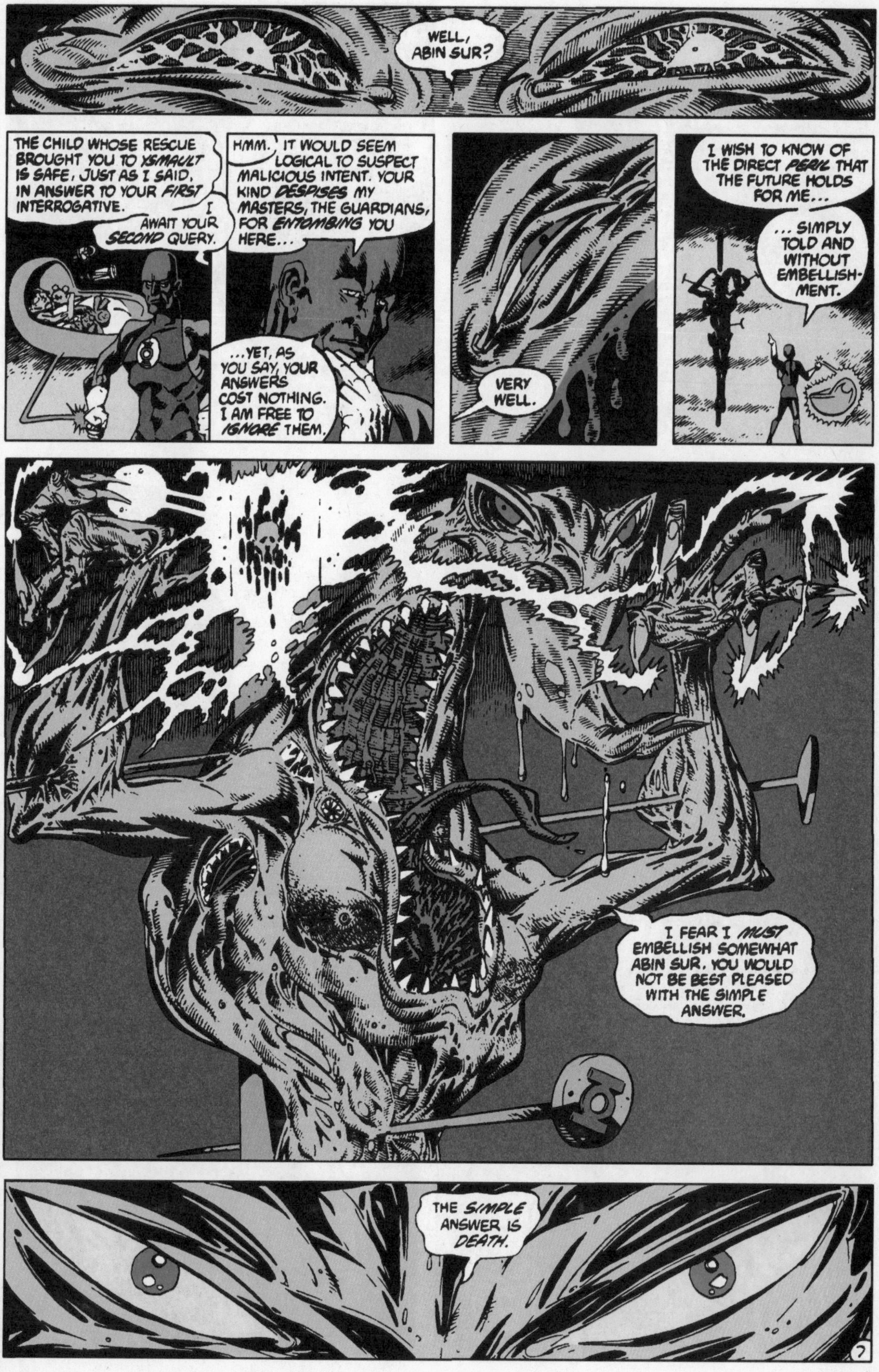

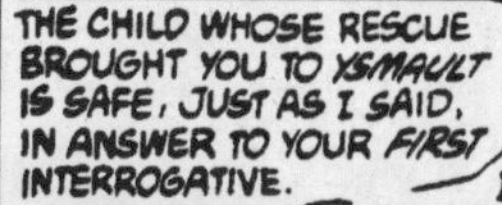
THE CHILD WHOSE RESCUE BROUGHT YOU TO *YSMAULT* IS SAFE, JUST AS I SAID, IN ANSWER TO YOUR *FIRST* INTERROGATIVE.
I AWAIT YOUR *SECOND* QUERY.

HMM. IT WOULD SEEM LOGICAL TO SUSPECT MALICIOUS INTENT. YOUR KIND *DESPISES* MY MASTERS, THE GUARDIANS, FOR *ENTOMBING* YOU HERE...
...YET, AS YOU SAY, YOUR ANSWERS COST NOTHING. I AM FREE TO *IGNORE* THEM.

VERY WELL.

I WISH TO KNOW OF THE DIRECT *PERIL* THAT THE FUTURE HOLDS FOR ME...
...SIMPLY TOLD AND WITHOUT EMBELLISH-MENT.
I FEAR I *MUST* EMBELLISH SOMEWHAT ABIN SUR. YOU WOULD NOT BE BEST PLEASED WITH THE SIMPLE ANSWER.

THE *SIMPLE* ANSWER IS *DEATH*.
7

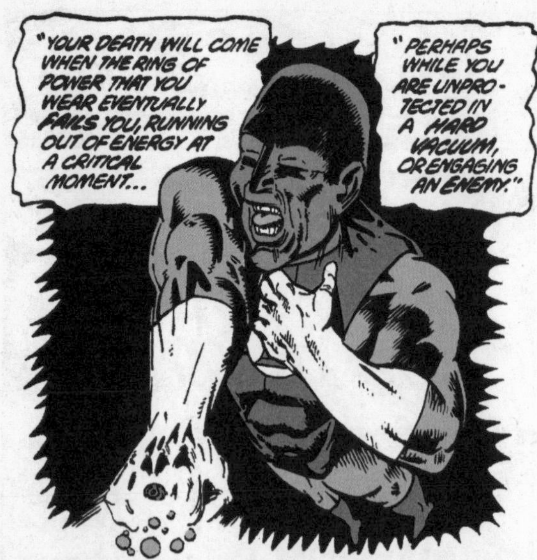
"YOUR DEATH WILL COME WHEN THE RING OF POWER THAT YOU WEAR EVENTUALLY FAILS YOU, RUNNING OUT OF ENERGY AT A CRITICAL MOMENT...
"PERHAPS WHILE YOU ARE UNPROTECTED IN A HARD VACUUM, OR ENGAGING AN ENEMY."

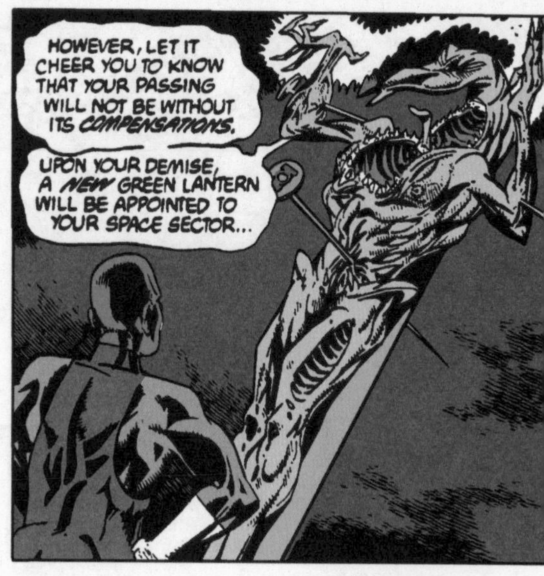
HOWEVER, LET IT CHEER YOU TO KNOW THAT YOUR PASSING WILL NOT BE WITHOUT ITS COMPENSATIONS.
UPON YOUR DEMISE, A NEW GREEN LANTERN WILL BE APPOINTED TO YOUR SPACE SECTOR...

"THROUGHOUT THE GREEN LANTERN CORPS HE SHALL BE HAILED AS GREATEST AMONGST HIS CONTEMPORARIES.
"WHEREVER HE GOES, LEGENDS SHALL SPRING UP IN HIS FOOTSTEPS... YOUR OWN ACHIEVEMENTS BEING UTTERLY ECLIPSED.
"DOES THAT BOTHER YOU?"

BOTHER ME?
WHAT AN AMUSING NOTION.
OF COURSE IT DOESN'T BOTHER ME... EVEN IN THE UNLIKELY EVENTUALITY THAT YOU SPEAK THE TRUTH.

BUT IT IS I WHO SHOULD ASK THE QUESTIONS...
WHAT IS THE MOST TERRIBLE CATASTROPHE THAT THE GREEN LANTERN CORPS, IN WHICH I SERVE, HAS YET TO FACE?
8

YOU SPEAK OF THE *FINAL* CATASTROPHE...
"AFTER UNTOLD MILLENNIA, THE ENEMIES OF THE GREEN LANTERN CORPS WILL RISE UNITED AGAINST THEM.
"THE CORPS SHALL BE DESTROYED TO THE LAST LIFE FORM. THE PLANET OA SHALL BE AS DUST.
"AMONGST THE GATHERED FOEMEN SHALL BE NUMBERED THE WEAPONERS OF QWARD, RANX THE SENTIENT CITY, AND THE UNSPEAKABLE CHILDREN OF THE WHITE LOBE.
"THE EMPIRE OF TEARS, FINALLY RELEASED FROM ENTOMBMENT, SHALL JOIN THE ASSAULT.
"SODAM YAT, A DAXAMITE HAILED AS THE ULTIMATE GREEN LANTERN, WILL PERISH BATTLING THE LOBE-SPAWN.
"THE PLANET-FORM GREEN LANTERN NAMED MOGO WILL BE LAST TO FALL, AS RANX EXPLODES A BLINK-BOMB WITHIN HIS CORE.
"AND AFTER THAT, THERE WILL ONLY BE THE DEMONS, DANCING IN THE RUINS OF OA TO THE RHYTHM OF DRUMS BOUND WITH TAUT BLUE SKIN."
9

YOU ARE WELL-NAMED, QULL OF THE FIVE INVERSIONS. YOU INVERT THE TRUTH RELENTLESSLY.
THIS TERRIBLE APOCALYPSE IS THE FRUIT OF A MIND SICK WITH FANTASIES OF REVENGE.

IF YOU SAY SO, ABIN SUR.
IN ANY EVENT, YOU HAVE MADE THE THREE ENQUIRIES PERMITTED TO YOU.
YOU MAY LEAVE YSMAULT AND FORGET ALL THAT I HAVE SAID.

BE ASSURED, DEMON, THAT IS MY PRECISE INTENTION.
FAREWELL TO YOU, AND TO THIS DISMAL WORLD THAT IS YOUR DUNGEON.
I LEAVE YOU TO YOUR IMAGININGS.

WELL, BROTHER QULL? HAVE YOU DESTROYED HIM?
IT WAS NO GREAT CHALLENGE. THE INTELLECTUAL ONES ARE ALWAYS THE EASIEST TO ENTANGLE...
...BUT YES, DEAR SISTER ROIXEAUME, I HAVE DESTROYED HIM...

...THOUGH IT WILL BE A DECADE BEFORE HE KNOWS IT.

...AND THE IMMORTAL DEMONS OF YSMAULT FOUND THEIR OWN LAUGHTER SO DISTRACTING A NOVELTY THAT THEY DID NOT CEASE FOR NINETEEN WEEKS.

ABIN SUR'S RUMINATIONS UPON THE MATTER ENDURED FAR LONGER...
HMM.

SO TELL ME... IS THERE A CHANCE THAT YOU MIGHT RUN OUT OF ENERGIES AT SOME VITAL INSTANT, IRRE-SPECTIVE OF WHETHER QULL LIED?
A REMOTE CHANCE, BUT YES...IT IS POSSIBLE.

THEN I CAN SEE NO HARM IN OBSERVING PRECAUTIONS. PERHAPS ON LONGER MISSIONS I SHOULD TRAVEL BY STARSHIP, CONSERVING YOUR ENERGIES?
I HAVE NO OBJECTION TO THIS PROPOSAL.

GOOD.
THEN I MAY PUT THE EMPIRE OF TEARS AND THEIR MORBID SPECULATIONS ENTIRELY FROM MY MIND.
INCIDENTALLY, IS IT NOT TIME THAT I RECHARGED YOU? YOU MUST BE LOW ON POWER...

YOU RECHARGED ME BUT AN HOUR AGO, ABIN SUR.

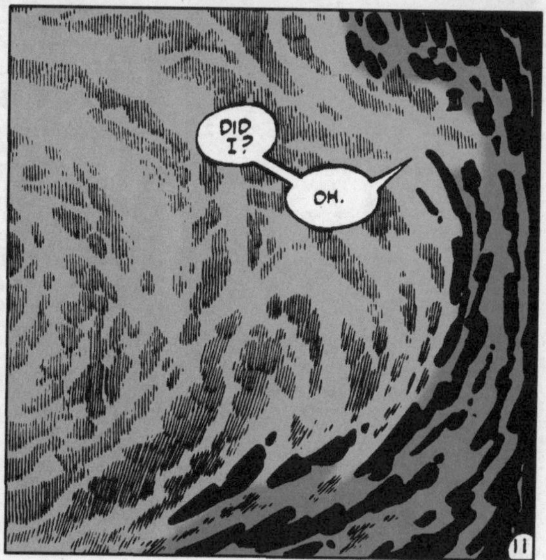
DID I?
OH.
11

EPILOGUE:

YEARS LATER, HE DIED.
THE YELLOW RADIATION GIRDLE ABOUT THE TURQUOISE PLANET RENDERED BOTH STARSHIP AND RING OF POWER USELESS WITHIN INSTANTS.
HE FELL.

IF ONLY HE'D RELIED UPON THE RING ALONE, HE MIGHT PERHAPS HAVE TESTED THE RADIATION BEFORE PLUNGING THROUGH IT.
IF ONLY...

THE SHIP'S GESTALT COMPLEX SHRIEKED ONCE, WENT HOPELESSLY INSANE, AND THEN MELTED.
HE TRIED TO RECALL WHAT HIS SUCCESSOR WOULD LOOK LIKE.
HE FELL...

...AND ALL THE WAY DOWN, IN HIS MIND, HE COULD HEAR THEM LAUGHING.
END